The End of the Island

The End of the Island

Finding Life in the Movements of
Human Suffering, Pain, and Loss

Jeffrey C. Tucker

RESOURCE *Publications* · Eugene, Oregon

THE END OF THE ISLAND
Finding Life in the Movements of Human Suffering, Pain, and Loss

Resource Publications
An Imprint of Wipf and Stock Publishers
199 W. 8th Ave., Suite 3
Eugene, OR 97401

www.wipfandstock.com

PAPERBACK ISBN: 978-1-4982-7906-2
HARDCOVER ISBN: 978-1-4982-7908-6

Manufactured in the U.S.A.

"It is too dark to see anymore. It is too heavy to hold onto. I am the canary in the coal mine and I am starting to choke."

—ANONYMOUS WRITING FOUND IN A
HOSPITAL CHAPEL PRAYER BOOK

The End of the Island is dedicated to the author of this moving, painful, and heartfelt cry . . . and to everyone who has ever felt the same way.

Contents

CONTENTS

Foreword

The Voice of the Author

My voice joins those of many others in the great mystery of life. It joins in the mystery of suffering and loss, as well. My voice is not immune. No voice is. But I have placed my voice in writing. I have put some words to the mystery of life, suffering, and loss in the face of my own pain and grief along the way. My voice speaks in the hope that the words that follow might matter to you. In the hope that these words might make a small difference in *your* suffering. That they might help you to think about your own suffering differently. That you might seek and find a life-affirming pathway within it. Perhaps this book can help.

I was raised as a child in a broken home. Not shattered, but broken. I was more than adequately provided for while I was growing up, but I lived with little outward affection or heartfelt love each day. There was little spontaneity in our home. Little involvement. I suppose that this, in turn, left a little hole in me that I've had to wrestle with throughout my adult life. That hole widened through the years, as I lost my brother to suicide as a young adult. While he was the youngest of my siblings, he may have felt the dysfunctions of our home most acutely. I have also lost my mother, father, stepfather, and great aunt to death during my own adult years. I have spoken at most of their funerals, eulogizing their lives while failing to properly process my own grief. I took the path of being strong for others in their losses. I am fairly quick with laughter and joyfulness along life's path. But tears have been harder to come by for me. Perhaps I never really learned how to cry.

While I have felt the stinging pain of loss, I have also been abundantly blessed. Blessed by my spouse and our two grown children. Blessed by our lives together in a loving, spontaneous, and involved home. Blessed by a long career in people coaching, consulting, and project leadership. But blessed most of all by a mid-life call to enter and complete seminary. An unexpected call by God. A call to study, research, and write extensively on contextual theology—where I learned that how we think about God and our suffering has much to do with our own cultures, histories, geographies, ethnicity, gender, and economic status. Our suffering is unique to each of us, shaped by myriad conscious and unconscious influences. This call has shaped me in ways that I understand and in ways that I don't yet.

Learning and writing about theology is a worthwhile endeavor. But it is not really where my heart lives. Once again, God knew that and subsequently called me to hospital chaplaincy. This is, perhaps, the most meaningful call yet in my life of faith. For it is here that I see human suffering as really lived in the lives of the countless patients and families I have ministered to. Through chaplaincy, I've been privileged to enter into a truly sacred space across virtually every faith tradition and sometimes none at all. This space is so profound as to resist any feeble effort to describe or define it on my part. But in this space, I have learned to see God differently. I have learned to listen with my heart, not just my ears and my mind. I have learned to pray in new ways with those who suffer. I have learned to let my own wounds heal, even as my heart literally breaks for the suffering of others. I have learned to open up about my own losses in life. I have learned to acknowledge and 'name' my own feelings. Most of all, though, I have learned to cry a bit. In the pages that follow, please allow my tears to join your own. More importantly, please allow the tears of a loving God join with those of each of us—bringing wisdom, strength, purpose, and even hope our way.

Introduction

Why does human suffering exist and persist? What is its purpose and meaning? Why can't we escape it? Why do others that I love so much get sick and die? And what about me? Everything was going so well until it wasn't. Everything was progressing nicely until it wasn't. Everyone was fine until it all changed. Why me? Why them? Why then? Why now? Why not some time later? Why not never? Ever.

But what if there were no suffering, pain, and loss? What would it be like to live without them? How would *we* be different, better off, or not really human as a consequence? How would our view of our life, our family and neighbors, or even the world change? Would we still need faith, a God, our worship community, or even prayer? What would taking a breath feel like if it never hurt to do so—if we could forever freely and easily breathe each one? Would the simple acts of human touch and embrace mean as much? Would we need and give compassion? What would it feel like to never need healing? How would the answers to life's most pressing questions be different if the questions of human suffering were never asked first?

And what would joy look like if not counterweighed by sorrow and anguish? Could we laugh and dance and sing if we could not also cry? What would light look like without the darkness of night? How would the warmth of spring feel without the biting cold of the winter that preceded it? How refreshing a cold glass of water without the prior dryness, heat, and sweat of exertion? If we could choose to make all suffering go away, would we therefore also choose not to live? Or would we choose to live forever in a blissful and unburdened state? What would that look like? What would I look like? How would others look to me?

There are so many deep, abiding questions. But human suffering, pain, and loss beg some initial, more practical questions than those above. When we are hurting for ourselves or for others, our esoteric questions are usually brushed aside, at least for the moment. That doesn't mean that they're unimportant ones. However, they are for later. Human pain isn't a theological or academic exercise. Our immediate and pressing questions are often quite *specific*. Among them:

- Where and why is my specific suffering or pain or loss?

- Where am *I* in this process of suffering and how did I get here?

- Who and where is the Divine in my suffering?

- Where is my human support to help me through it?

- Where is my ultimate hope and deliverance from it?

- And how can I find specific help right here and now where I need it most? Right here. Right now.

If you breathe and walk and live, you've likely asked these kinds of questions. Perhaps you're asking them at this very moment. I have asked these questions and I still do. In some respects, I've found some helpful direction—for myself and for others. What I've not found are rigid, full-proof, one-size-fits-all answers. So, if you're looking for a neat and tidy self-help book, this may not be the place for you. What I *can* offer you is this: an opportunity to look at your suffering with a fresh set of eyes. A chance to see God's loving movement and presence *within* your suffering. To better see life-giving and sustaining movement in this space. To 'be' more whole, heal, and transform while you're suffering amidst your pain. To make today matter, even when tomorrow is unclear. To invite others to walk with you, wherever your suffering takes you.

In this book, I strive to walk with you in your suffering. To move with you. If we move together, we might just find some helpful answers along the path, not simply more questions. In truth, we will never find 'the' answer, though. There may be many. And they may not come all at once. They may even seem to compete at times. And frankly, we will never fully 'arrive'. The totality of *all* our questions will never be resolved completely. For remember, I am talking here about movement— not a neat, linear journey.

Having said that, let's try. In the chapters that follow, I will do my best to realistically and honestly address each of the *specific* questions most often raised in situations of human suffering. I'll draw on a number of sources: my own life experiences, contexts, and movements; my Christian faith; my work as a hospital chaplain; my theological education, research, and writing; other faith traditions and theologies; pastoral thinking; creative literature; just plain ideas; and an intriguing story about an island. As you can see, I'll cast a wide and inclusive net. And I'll write in a different kind of way. A form of narrative poetry. With a fresh edge. With some humor where it fits. In short, concise, and focused 'bites' that we can digest more easily. In language that we actually speak. Directed to not only Christians, but to all. And with some challenge for all, as well.

For movement implies a willingness to stay curious and open, to experience some shifts on your part, to stretch, to learn, and to reflect. The ideas in this book have pushed some real boundaries for me— and I trust they'll nudge yours, as well. Along the way, my hope and prayer for you is this: that you might find peace, comfort, grace, strength, meaning, and even 'new life' in the movements of your life, even those found in your suffering. So let's get moving and see where it takes us. And let's see if we can discover something about *The End of the Island* in the process. How about starting right here? How about now? Join me, please . . .

Chapter One

Seeking the End of the Island

"For after all the great religions have been preached and expounded, or have been revealed by brilliant scholars, or have been written in fine books and embellished in fine language with finer covers, man—all man—is still confronted with the Great Mystery."

—CHIEF LUTHER STANDING BEAR

Movement One:
Introducing the Story

An elderly man painfully disembarked from a small boat onto an island. His journey had been long and arduous. The seas had been rough throughout the passage. He had been jostled violently around the deck onboard the boat, bounding from beam to beam. The craft had listed severely to its side, as it rocked on the impact of cresting waves. It struggled to climb each crest, only to careen down a towering slide of water into the next trough. The wind howled, sending a cold, biting spray of seawater onto his wrinkled, worn face. Gray, foreboding skies melted into the darker, gray, and menacing waters below. The old man had tried to fix a gaze to the horizon in order to steady himself. But the sky and sea were indistinguishable. He could make out only the white froth of the violent waters as they surrounded the small boat.

Bruised, tired, and sick from the trip, the old man was nonetheless glad for more solid footing now. The island's sand, rocks, and dirt steadied his body. The faint sunlight between the menacing clouds would dry his wet clothing in the hours ahead. The surrounding trees provided shelter from the wind, easing its bite on his face. Although worse for the wear, he consoled himself with this fact: He had completed the passage. He had finally arrived. His keen and abiding sense of his loneliness, pain, loss, and suffering abated, even if only for the moment. Relief was a welcome thing, he thought. He felt, as well, a tingling sense of hope. For the first time in many, many years, he felt almost 'alive'. His tired, frail body now seemed to move with a slightly lighter step. He resolved to locate the end of the island, where he would find the answer to his suffering. "I am almost there," the old man said to himself. "Just a little longer . . . "

He glanced around to set his bearings. There were no roads, signs, or other markers. Only a path. It was dirt-covered and uneven. Growth bordered each side of this narrow trail. The old man was suddenly gripped with a momentary fear. He had strength only to find the end of the island—nothing more. There was neither time nor energy for getting lost, making side-trips, or encountering distractions. What if he didn't find the end? What if he died before getting the answer that he needed? The man shuddered as he contemplated the thought of dying alone, forsaken, and with no understanding of his suffering.

For a moment, he thought about turning around. He could return home by the same boat that had brought him here. At least, he thought, he would die in his own bed. But as the old man turned around, he sighed with resignation. The boat was now gone. Tears began to stream down the deeply etched ruts on his worn face. He had cried so much over these past, difficult years. He was surprised to have any tears left. He was now faced with this truth: there was no way back and apparently no way forward. The old man leaned against a tree, sighed deeply, and crouched to the ground. He was discouraged and exhausted.

He must have dozed for some time. The old man awoke hours later, startled by a gentle nudge of a stranger. His eyesight was nearly gone, and he could only faintly make out the outlines of the person. But her voice was calm and assured, putting him more at ease. She helped the man slowly to his feet and steadied him against a low-lying limb of a nearby tree. She asked him if he was all right? Asked what he was seeking? He replied quickly, "I am here to find the end of the island. I'm told that this place holds the answer to my suffering and pain. It is only at the end of this strange place that my suffering may finally make some sense to me. It is only there that I can truly understand and die in peace. Time is short. Please help me find it."

The woman reflected for a moment. She looked a bit bemused, but didn't want to be impolite. She then smiled and said, "What if you've already found it?" "Where?" the old man asked back. "Here," the woman replied, in turn. The old man scanned the island. It was small and somewhat barren to the naked eye. A bit incredulously, he said, "No, this is not it. I know it. I need to find the end of the island. That will be the place. At the end of this island." "So be it," the woman returned. The old man's gaze returned to the island's horizon and he inquired, "I am lost and don't know where it is. Is there a map of this place? Is there a guide who can lead me? I am alone and scared. I'm slow of foot and low of energy. Time is short. What is the most direct route to get me there?"

The woman reflected again, this time a bit longer. The old man wondered what she was thinking. He was growing ever more tired and impatient. She sensed his urgency and pointed to the path ahead. She offered, "Take that path." The man was unsure. It seemed like such a nondescript way of reaching such an important place. But it was the only path that he could see. He reluctantly thanked her and turned away to proceed. Then, he hesitated briefly to ask, "Will this path take me to the end of the island? Is it a direct route? If not, how do I know which turns to make? And how do I know when I've reached the end of the island?" The woman approached the man and gently patted his shoulder. She nudged him toward the path and replied, "Simply start. Stay open and mindful. You will learn as you continue moving. Trust in yourself. Listen to those things and people you encounter as you move. You are not alone, even when you think you are." The woman extended her hand to him. He took it and held it tightly for a moment. Then, he released her hand and headed haltingly to the trail ahead.

Chapter Two

Where is my Suffering?

"There is the solitude of suffering, when you go through darkness that is lonely, intense, and terrible. Words become powerless to express your pain; what others hear from your words is so distant and different from what you are actually suffering."

—JOHN O'DONOHUE

Pre-Movement Stretch

Human suffering changes everything. It dislodges us from our spaces of comfort, stability, surety, and knowing. It cuts our anchors from tomorrow's promise, today's expectations, and the grounding of yesterday. It severs the connections from our hopes from their actual fulfillment. The things that we hold most closely are dis-attached from our withering grasp. It can be a dark, lonely, and helpless feeling space for us. In the pages ahead, we'll honestly acknowledge, honor, and discuss the losses of suffering. But we'll also explore another way. Where we face our suffering with a healthier sense of our own human finiteness. Where we might find ways to better accept the randomness of our life. Where we might hold onto things less tightly. Where we might simply 'be' in the movement of our pain and sorrow—instead of only seeking ways to run from it. And doing so in ways that integrate *all* elements of our lives (including our pain) more holistically into the loved, special persons that we are.

Movement One:
Against the Gale

The old man awoke on the path the next morning. The evening before had been calm and warm. The new day, however, was notably marked by stronger winds and darkening skies. He struggled to move against the sheer force of the air. It pounded and pummeled his body, pushing his withered skin against his fragile ribs. Each new step exerted strenuous resistance. The man tried in vain to cover his eyes from the wind's onslaught. He found the path rocky, and struggled to clearly see the way ahead. So, he kept his eyes facing forward as best as he could. As the man made a narrow turn in the path, he came upon another person.

Briefly startled, the old man regained his composure and asked the stranger, "Do you know the way to the end of the island? I need to find it soon, as I need to know the answer to my questions." The stranger asked, "What questions are you seeking clarity on?" The old man replied with some urgency. "Why I suffer and live in pain." They stood together in silence for some time. The void became quite awkward for the old man. The stranger sensed this and offered, "Last evening, the stars literally burst out of the sky. There was not a cloud to be seen. The moon gently bathed the ground with enough light to move by. Everything danced in a wonderful silhouette. The breeze was warm and comforting. I had high expectations for today, as well. I gave away my coat to another stranger, thinking that I wouldn't need it today. But it now turns out that I do." The old man, now curious, asked in return, "So what will you wear today to keep you warm in this gale?" The stranger replied simply, "Nothing is forever. That includes my coat.

In fact, someone gave it to me a few days back. I didn't own it. Now, someone else does until he doesn't."

The old man was, by now, quite perplexed and worried. He mused, "But if you knew that the strong winds would return today, would you have given the coat away last evening? What you thought to be true didn't turn out that way." The stranger smiled and said, "The thing is that I *didn't* know. I never know what tomorrow will bring. I don't hold onto things. When I did in the past, the things became ragged and worn. And they weighed me down. Then sometimes, they disappeared altogether. Besides, I travel more nimbly without them."

The old man was concerned and asked, "But how will you stay warm?" The stranger replied, "The more you move, the warmer you become. The trick is to keep moving. I'll face tomorrow's weather when it comes, whatever it may bring. Besides, I find that the rocks and ledges along the way nicely break the force of the winds. That is good enough. They, unlike the other things, were always there and they always will be. And I don't have to carry them. "The old man was now confused. Today looked so promising . . . . yesterday. But today it doesn't. He then turned into the gale and continued to walk. After a bit, he stopped under a ledge on the path. It was much calmer and dryer there. He began to feel too warm and briefly removed his own coat. Then he walked onto the next protected cover some ways down the trail.

Movement Two:
Future Promise

We all look to the future to one extent or another.

We think about tomorrow. What's coming. What's on the way. Just around the corner.

We muse on its promise. Its hope. Its allure.

So when we reflect on our progress, it's not just *from* some-where . . . . It's on the way *to* somewhere better. Way better. So, so, so much better.

And in order to get to the better, we dream, we plan, we strive, we work.

Always looking straight ahead. To the way-more hopeful spot. Way-more . . .

We pray, we wish on stars, we cross our fingers, we look to the horizon, we practice our best good luck charms. We fret, we scheme, we promise to do this, if only that.

We say things like "See you down the road; let's do that next time; when I grow up; when I retire; when I arrive; later..."

We count our blessings, with an eye to the next ones coming someday soon.

We do all these things because tomorrow matters.

Our future matters. The one just down the road. The promise of tomorrow. Remember?

It matters to us, to our families, our friends, our co-workers, our faith communities.

It matters to the whole world, to all creation, or so it seems.

The promises of tomorrow call us, beckon us, prod us, push us, work us, and promise us.

Until they no longer seem to.

Until we suffer. Until we're in pain. Until we lose someone important to our hearts.

Until tomorrow's promise crashes headlong. Smash. Boom.

Into the wreck of loss and pain today. Our wreck.

Movement Three:
Current Expectations

We're somebody in this very moment. We matter. No, we really matter . . .

We're unique and special right this second. Or at least we feel that we are.

We mark out our identities in this space called 'today'. "Yep, X marks the spot."

And, sometimes, we invite others to join us. You know, to *our* X spot. Ours.

We were created to be joyful. Like we've earned the right. Now. Hard fought. Bring it.

And we live life to the fullest with a sense of urgency. "Gotta move. Time's a wastin.'"

Furthermore, we deserve to be happy in the moment. Isn't that why we're here, anyway?

We pray for blessings today, right now, this instant, for the rest of the day.

We check on the current news, the current weather, the current scene, the current fashion.

The current trends, the current culture. At least how they impact me . . . Currently.

We build our current assets, our current savings, our current possessions, our current circle of friends. Our current stuff. Gotta have that stuff. Currently.

We fret about today, for tomorrow is later. "Don't swim against the current 'current.'"

We celebrate this moment, this time, this event, this friendship, this thing.

We count our blessings, with an eye to the next ones coming a little later today.

We do these things because today matters. Our currency is now.

'Now' matters to us, to our families, our friends, our co-workers, our faith communities.

It matters to the whole world, to all creation, or so it seems.

The expectations of today call us, beckon us, prod us, push us, work us, and settle in us.

Until they no longer seem to.

Until we suffer. Until we're in pain. Until we lose someone important to our hearts.

Until today turns into a mess. A big one, at that. Currently.

Movement Four:
Past Memories

We look to the past. We remember. We mark those things now gone by.

We muse on our past accomplishments, our memories, our stories, our lives, our youth.

We fondly recall our vacations, our travels, our holidays, our celebrations, and our family gatherings. "Here, let me show you my pictures. I have only three hundred or so."

We look back on things we've owned, things we've sold, things we've traded, things we've lost, and things we let go. The things we said 'see ya' to.

We say things like, "when I was younger; when I was stronger; when I was your age . . . "

We recall the good old days, the better times, the best of times, the worst of times.

We remember the times when things were easier, harder, slower, faster. They just were.

We muse on the things we did. The things we didn't do after all. The things we only talked about. The things in the past we kept secret from everyone else.

We look back to measure our present and our future.

We look back to ground us more firmly now.

We look back to make sense of today and to learn for tomorrow.

We do all these things because our past matters. So do our memories of the past.

They matter to us, to our families, our friends, our co-workers, our faith communities.

They matter to the whole world, to all creation, or so it seems.

Past memories call us, beckon us, teach us, push us, orient us, and sustain us.

Until they no longer seem to.

Until we suffer. Until we're in pain. Until we lose someone important to our hearts.

Until the past becomes a burden or chain. A source of continued suffering and sorrow.

Or something we'd rather forget about. Or ditch in the ditch.

Movement Five:
The Non-Fulfillment Gap

Suffering is like a void, a crack, a fissure, a chasm.

It's a major disconnect, a gap, a missing link, a blacking out, an empty space, a shorted circuit. It's like a giant sinkhole that we're falling into. Without a ladder. Stuck.

It's a future promise unfilled. It's a current expectation never met.

It's a past memory lost, forgotten, diluted, churned, smashed, blurred, or splattered.

It's today's hope dashed. Today's plan trashed. Soiled. Dumped. Ruined.

It smashed and crashed and wrecked tomorrow. It's 'totaled'. Without insurance.

It cast off yesterday like a rudderless ship. Or one that keeps crashing on me now.

It left today with nothing. Rained out. Cancelled, not postponed. No rain check, either.

It's stolen my plans, my relationships, my things, my home, my savings, my loves.

It's broken into my life in the darkness of night, and I never saw it coming.

Or maybe I saw it coming after all, but it's still not right or fair.

In fact, it's not fair at all. In fact, it stinks. In every foul way possible.

It's betrayed my trust, my faith, my sense of continuity, and my view of the sacred.

It has cost me something, everything, nearly all that I had saved. It took all I had left.

It's drained me, suffocated me, choked me, and stifled me.

"I don't deserve this. Not any of this. Not one iota of this. Nada."

"Why this thing, why this time, why me? Why me?"

"Why me now? Why me here? Why me at all? Why not someone else for a change?"

I didn't deserve it. I worked hard to prevent it. I worked even harder to make it go away.

But it didn't. And it's left me unfulfilled. In the gap.

Empty, lost, and alone. In the gap. But only worse. In the barren canyon.

Movement Six:
The Affect

Suffering is like an unquenchable hunger or thirst. It never seems to go away.

It makes cold, fresh water taste bitter in my mouth. Like I want to spit it right out.

It wakes me in the night in pain. And I can't get back to sleep. So, I pace the floors.

It makes me shake to my bones. Out of fear and misery. Out of my mind.

It leaves me alone when I need someone by my side to comfort me. All by myself.

It leaves ugly scars on my body, my heart, and my soul. The kind that never heal.

It leaves me without control—over who, the how, the when, and the why. All of it.

It makes me feel marginalized, as if people were talking about me, not to me.

It makes me feel pitied, not loved or wanted anymore. Just pitied . . . for my 'condition'.

It brings me rejection as someone not well, not normal, not adjusting, not accepting enough. Because of my illness, my disease. My 'condition'.

It completely and utterly confuses me. Disorients me.

Like a ship blown off its mooring; a plane without a tail fin; a car without a steering wheel; a trip without my GPS. Really lost . . . in my 'condition'.

I'm a bundle of regrets, disappointments, and setbacks.

I am loathed to hope, as tomorrow may bring only more sorrow.

I can no longer recall a time when I was able to do that thing or go to that place without help, without tears, and without fears.

I can't recall when a day was simply a typical day. Without my 'condition'.

I can't recall the names of those no longer in my life . . . because of my 'condition'.

Perhaps they got tired of me, my sickness, my pain, my loss, or the grind of it all.

Perhaps they simply wore out, just like me. In my 'condition'.

Movement Seven:
The Effect

When I suffer, I want to *Fight*:

For all I'm worth. To win this thing.

For even one more good day.

For my dignity.

Or because others think that I should. Or say that I should.

When I suffer, I want to *Retreat*:

To fall back.

To run and hide.

To stay under my covers in bed all day. Everyday.

To be alone . . . or to resent being alone yet again.

When I suffer, I want to be *Angry*:

At others for this.

At myself for this.

At this thing, this creature, this uninvited guest of mine, this travesty, this tragedy, this invasion of my life or body.

At anything and everything. And sometimes at nothing. But I'm still angry at it.

When I suffer, I want to *Surrender*:

To the battle, for I am desperately tired.

Just for today.

For the moment only . . . to take a short breather.

In order to live to fight the battle again tomorrow.

Movement Eight:
Grieving our Attachments

Suffering is grieving my pain. Grieving my very suffering, itself.

It's grieving my sorrows, my setbacks, my emptiness, and my unworthiness.

But I most grieve my losses. There are many, many losses these days.

Because I suffer, I lose things. Because I have lost things, I now suffer.

I grieve the loss of my attachments in life—the drip, drip, dripping away of things I value.

I suffer the loss of the status quo, the steadiness, the comfortable sameness.

I've now lost my things, my identity, my place, my space, my things, my stuff.

I've lost my friends, my family, my neighbors, my helpers.

I've lost my security, my mobility, my serenity, and my seniority.

I've lost the answers to my problems, and sometimes even the right questions.

My hold on things, places, people, concepts, and solutions is more elusive than ever.

These things are coming loose from my weakened hands and grip. Really quickly now.

The losses slip slowly but steadily out of my life . . .

Like grains of sand in an hourglass. Rushing out of it now. Really quickly these days.

Like the drip of a water faucet. Pouring out of it now. Literally running.

Like the incremental setting of the sun. Speeding into dusk right now. Smashing down.

Like an ever changing landscape that I beg to sit still. That won't right now.

The losses pile up on me. They simply accumulate in my life. Right now.

Day-in, Day-out. Another small loss. And it's now become a big one. A big hole.

So, I grieve the things that were, but are no more. I grieve the losses most of all.

But what if doing so is all right after all?

Not just all right, but really part of it all. Part of my movement.

Movement Nine:
Another Way—New Vocabulary

"I am totally messed up. I hurt really bad. This whole situation is really bad."

Silence. Then, more silence. Then things get even worse because no one understands.

"Why don't they understand what this bad stuff is? My really bad. Cause it's bad."

"Why don't they understand how I'm feeling in the midst of this bad?"

"They tell me a lot that they 'understand'. No they don't. How could they?"

Part of what makes our suffering truly bad is that we suffer without words.

Our suffering vocabulary is really bad. We can do it to ourselves. Badly.

We grasp desperately for the words that might help ourselves and others to actually help.

The 'feeling' words. The words that sit directly underneath the unsaid bad stuff.

It's like a large iceberg. We see what sits on top of the water. The bad stuff.

But the bad stuff isn't what's really happening to us. It's frozen.

The stuff under the water is what sinks us. The non-verbalized 'feeling' stuff.

Like "I'm angry at this pain. I'm angry with the doctors today. I'm mad at myself."

Like "I'm sad that this has ruined our plans today. I'm sad that I can't be with you."

Like "I'm lonely laying here in the hospital. I'm feeling isolated and cut off."

Like "I'm afraid that I'm going to die. I am so fearful that I'll get bad news today."

Like "I'm anxious about all these doctors poking me. About the operation tomorrow."

Like "I'm glad that you came by to see me today. But I'm tired and need to rest now."

The feeling words are hard to find sometimes. And even harder to use.

Because they can make us feel vulnerable. Make us let down our guard as we power through the bad. But what if that's exactly what we need to do?

To help melt the bad iceberg. With the help of others.

Movement Ten:
Another Way—Accepting Our Finiteness

"I am mortal and finite." There, I said it. It was tough, but I said it.

"I wasn't created to live forever, to go on indefinitely, to take a place permanently here."

There, I said it again. It was really, really hard, but I said it.

That doesn't mean that I'm unloved by God, unworthy, unimportant, or not special.

It means that I've been born to live here for only awhile.

I formed in my mother's womb before I was born. I'm still forming.

When I'm gone from here, I'll still be forming. Somewhere else.

And not just me. It's everything in our midst, as well.

Creation is also birthing, developing, stretching, groaning, changing . . . and dying.

Look around you. Small, light green spring leaves turn deeper and larger in the summer. They turn brilliant red and orange and yellow in the autumn. Only to die in the winter. Not really dead, but feeding and tilling the soil for next spring.

Life is a cycle everywhere. In all of nature. We're not exempt. We are finite too.

All things bend against the heavy winds, the storms, the lashing rain, the cold air of life.

All life begins with the promise of an end . . . at least in its present form.

But what if that 'end' was just a beginning of something else?

Something new, something wonderful. Something more amazing for all creation.

What if life and death were building something, growing into something.

Combining into something? Or simply Becoming.

What if our mortality was a marvelous building block?

Not a death sentence . . . .

Movement Eleven:
Another Way—Accepting Randomness

Stuff happens. Sometimes bad stuff happens. Sometimes the truly awful stuff.

Sometimes for no apparent reason. None whatsoever as far as we can tell.

Sometimes we're in the wrong place at the wrong time.

Sometimes nature erupts and changes and churns . . . and we're smack in the middle of it.

Sometimes people make bad choices . . . and we get in the way of it.

Sometimes we make bad choices . . . and we pay for it.

Sometimes people make bad choices for us . . . and we suffer for it.

Sometimes people oppress other people . . . and we were born into it.

Sometimes people marginalize us . . . and we can't break away from it.

Sometimes we never saw it coming . . . and we were caught up in it.

Sometimes we saw it coming . . . but we couldn't run fast enough from it.

Sometimes it never even came . . . and we simply waited in vain for it.

Sometimes it never even started . . . and we quit waiting.

Life is infused with randomness. Sometimes stuff simply happens.

Good stuff, bad stuff, awful stuff, and in-between stuff.

It happens to good people, bad people, in-between people, and all people.

It happens to rich people, poor people, in-between people, and all people.

What if we accepted randomness as a part of life's journey?

Sometimes things have a good reason. Sometimes they simply don't.

Life's mystery and beauty invoke randomness. It's not always a curse or a blessing.

Sometimes it means that we are simply in motion.

We're moving . . .

Movement Twelve:
Another Way—Simply Being in the Movement

You probably thought I was going to say, "Simply being in the *moment.*"

And the next thing you know, you'd be meditating in the midst of your pain.

And you'd blank all things out of your mind. Except perhaps for an image.

And you'd sit in silence, listening to yourself breathe. And someone would say, "Breathe in, breathe out. Breathe in, breathe out. Make the breaths deep from your diaphragm, not your throat. That's it. Now, if your mind wanders, it's OK. Just bring yourself back to that word or object that your mind is focused on. You can open your eyes now. Our time is up, thank you."

Don't get me wrong. Meditation is a good thing. Being mindful and 'in the moment' is constructive, relaxing, and mind focusing.

"But don't they know that I'm in pain? That I'm suffering? That I'm grieving? That my mind is already numb. My view is already dark enough. Why would I want more of the same?"

So, here's another way: What if you sat quietly with your eyes wide open, looking around your space with your keenest sense of vision, looking for goodness and love in your very midst? What if you actually heightened your senses, discovering the little things around you: the smile on his face, the sound of her laughter, the warmth of human touch, the look of a caring eye, the security of a hug, the softness of your pillow, the light of day outside your door, the voice of a child, the breeze on your neck, the beauty of a flower . . .

What if you looked for the blessed movement of things and gently entered into them?

What if you moved about *in* them for a while? Took some peace *from* them?

What if you found God's love, peace, grace, and comfort there? Right there and then.

Post-Movement Reflection Questions

How has my suffering most unhinged my own sense of time, place, and being?

What are the biggest losses in my life caused by my suffering?

How has my suffering impacted my expectations for my future and that of those whom I love?

What attachments do I hold onto most tightly? Which can I loosen my grip on in order to better equip me to move through my suffering?

What areas of inner peace can I work to achieve today, even in the face of my suffering?

Post-Movement Rest and Prayer

Thank you, loving God, for the *real* promise of our lives. The promise that, in all things, you are forever. You are permanent. Your love is unceasing, transcending, and everlasting. May I hold firmly to that love, God, in my pain, sorrow, loss, and suffering. Might the disorientation and dislocation of my suffering be countered by your solid presence. The rock of your foundation. Your ledge that protects me from the utter hopelessness of this raging storm around me. Even as I lose the things that I've so valued, might you fill me with more lasting things. In the process, help me to walk this path of suffering with newfound peace, built firmly in the grasp of your loving arms. Help me to better accept my own mortality, the randomness of things, the things that I can't understand. Help me to simply be in your 'moment', your movement. In your loving, caring, healing embrace. Thank you, God.

Chapter Three

Where am I in my Suffering?

"It is painfully easy to define human beings. They are beings who, for no reason at all, create their own unnecessary suffering."

—Sōseki Natsume

Pre-Movement Stretch

When we're hurting and suffering, it's not just about the pain and loss. It's about who and where we are in the midst of it, as well. Pain encloses us. Isolates us. Make us feel more alone and forsaken. Leaves us feeling like we've 'become' our disease. In the pages ahead, we'll explore ways in which we've long been cutting ourselves off. From us and from others. From our true identities as loved beings. For many, we've lived our entire lives untethered and existentially alone. Long before the suffering began. Cast off from the very sources of comfort, support, and love that we need to flourish—especially when we subsequently suffer. And we have largely done it to ourselves. God is not responsible. We'll discuss the roots of our dis-attachment: our notions of sin, our 'seeking', the unworthiness label that we accept from others, the shortcomings of our very religions. And we'll look at another way. A potentially healthier way. Where we can read our religious books with another lens. Where we can look more broadly for God's word and spirit in our world. Where we can walk in others' shoes, in other places, and through the eyes of others along the way. We'll do so in the hope that these movements might bring new ways of looking at ourselves, our suffering, our place with others, and at God's expansive, present love. For God is still speaking with us. God still loves us. Even when we don't love ourselves.

Movement One:
The Lonely Path

The old man awoke under the shade of a protective rock ledge. He felt better, having slept soundly through the night. The wind and rain had battered the ground, but he had stayed dry. He rubbed his eyes and tried to focus—still groggy and lethargic. The sun was slowly coming up on the horizon. The rays splintered toward him in uneven gleams of light, shooting through gaps in the thick trees and brush of the island. It would be hot today, he thought to himself. Best to get an early start before the sun gets higher in the sky.

He rose slowly and gingerly, feeling the stiffness in his bones. The ground had been hard under his frail body, but it had been dry. The old man was thankful for that much. He shook the dirt off his shoes and eased them back onto his aching feet. The wall of the ledge helped to steady his body, while he bent over to fit the shoes more snugly. He could feel a blister forming on his right ankle. "All this walking . . . ," he said to himself. He glanced around to secure his bearings, and headed for the path. Today, he thought. Perhaps, today I'll find the end of the island.

By midmorning, the temperature had risen markedly. It was humid and sticky. Salty sweat began to form and run into his eyes. They began to sting. The old man wiped his brow and pushed on. He thought about how lonely he was. For the first time, he felt truly alone. The path was showered with life and bloom and flowers. But he felt alone, nonetheless. As he turned a corner, he was startled by a stranger who walked toward him. The old man was glad for someone to talk to. He asked the stranger, "Is this the way to the end of the island?" The stranger looked back quizzically and replied, "Why do you travel this path alone?" The old man was now frustrated. "You didn't answer my question," he said. The stranger came back, "Why do you travel this path alone? There are many things to accompany you. There's life everywhere. There are things and plants and water and skies and animals and even people to walk with you."

The old man thought briefly about this. He responded, "I have to find the end of the island. It is there that I'll find the answers to my suffering. Time is short, and I need to move on. I have to do this thing. I can find the answer myself if only I can find the end of the island. I've made it this far on my own. I can finish this thing on my own. Now I'd like to talk to you more, but I must be moving on." He turned to walk on, but hesitated. Then he said to the stranger, "You, too, are alone. Yet you don't look so lonely as I. Who are your friends on this godforsaken island?" The stranger approached the old man and extended his hand. "You are, old man. You are. And so are many things and people. I let other things walk with me, to speak to me, to listen to me along the way. I find friendship in each day, whatever it brings. I am never alone." The old man shook the hand of the stranger. The stranger placed a blooming flower in the old man's hand. "Take this," the stranger said. "Walk with it today. You don't need to do everything today. You need not do it all yourself. You need not do it alone." The old man thanked the stranger and continued moving.

Movement Two:
Our Lonely Origins

You've heard it from the very beginning. "*You're* a sinner in need of forgiveness." Wait for it . . . . Wait . . . "Yes, you are a sinner. A sinner from the very beginning of time."

There, you heard it again. Probably for the umpteenth time.

"You were created as a fallen body, you know. Yes, fallen.

You were literally born into it. It's your shared inheritance.

Your body is inherently sinful. Now, your spirit is divine. But not the body. No chance.

Your body is flesh. Flesh that's rotten to the core, actually. Like Adam's.

Yes, and flesh is sinful. The worst kind of sinful, actually. Like Eve's.

Yes, and from the beginning. All the way back. To the Garden of Eden. Remember?

Yes, and you *will* eventually pay for it. It's foreordained. You know, cause and effect."

I heard it, and it registered subconsciously with me. Deeper than I thought, I guess.

But it really didn't feel so lonely on this path . . . until I started suffering.

Until I realized that my sinfulness caused all this suffering. Ah yes, I remember now.

"So, I guess I had it coming after all. I guess I had it coming. My bad is now *my* bad."

"I guess I've carried it with me all along. From the beginning. My inheritance."

"I guess it makes me a rotten person. In need of punishment, judgment, and bad things."

"I'm in need of a major 'time out' . . . unless I do and say certain things each week."

"Gee, I feel so guilty now. I guess I've had it coming to me after all. My bad."

So, here's a question: Why did God create me all messed up from the start?

Why did God place this burden on me? I wouldn't have done it to me. Or to others . . .

If God loves me, why did he create me as a sinner? From the Start? My inheritance?

But what if God didn't and we did it to *ourselves*? What if there's another way?

Movement Three:
Our Lonely Definitions

"In fact, you're not only a sinner . . . you have now become your disease."

When you suffer, you seem to become what ails you most. Actually morph into it.

It's like I had my disease from the very beginning . . . along with my sin.

"Hi, I'm Marilyn. I have cancer. Sometimes I feel like I'm only my cancer."

"Hi, I'm Peter. I've been disabled from birth. Sometimes I feel like a cripple. Sometimes I think others call me that name behind my back."

"Hi, I'm nobody important other than my disease, thank you. Sometimes, I feel like I *am* my tumor, my incision, my pain, my clotting, my depression, and my grief. I think I've forgotten who I really am. Drawn a blank on the actual 'me' underneath this mess."

It wasn't so lonely on this path until my suffering became 'me'.

Until my pain silently and slowly crept into me and stole my name, my identity.

Until my grief and loss began to define me as a person.

Why didn't it listen when I asked it to leave me alone?

Why didn't it let me live with my real name? My real 'me'.

Why don't others see me anymore as 'me'—not just my sickness?

Why don't others stop telling me that it'll all go away . . . it'll all get better soon?

Like I am less of a person with this disease.

Like I need all this to disappear if I am ever to be worthy again.

Like I can rejoin my life, my friends, my fellow worshippers when this evil in me leaves.

And why did God let this happen? You know, the naming 'me' after the disease thing.

But what if God didn't do this after all? What if we did it to ourselves?

What if there's another way? To get my real name, my real 'me' name back.

Movement Four:
Our Lonely Destinations

"I am really on the way now. Watch me.

Watch me run. Watch me run fast. Watch me run very, very fast.

Watch me strive, strive hard, strive harder, strive hardest.

Watch me win. Watch me win big. Watch me win everything. I'm en-'titled'.

Watch me arrive. Watch me relish arriving. Watch me staying on top after arriving.

Watch me make the rules, own the rules, rule the rules, adjudicate the rules.

Watch me on the podium of life. Watch me take home *all* the medals.

All by myself. I did it . . . I actually did it . . . I knew I could do it . . . all by myself.

Sorry, but I'm busy right now. I've figured it all out on my own, thank you.

What's that you ask: about being, relating, connecting, interdependence, linking?

Thanks, but I've got this thing all covered by my self-contained little self."

"Oops . . . now watch me slow down.

Watch me fall behind.

Watch me fall to the ground in pain and sorrow. What's happening here? What about the finish line?"

It didn't seem so lonely on this path while I was striving and arriving and achieving and winning. And staying on top. And making up the rules for me and for others.

But then it happened: the adrenalin stopped. The crowd went home. The cheers silenced.

And then it happened: the open world closed in on me. The rush became a void.

I had the world by the tail, until I didn't. I had it made until my thing 'made me'.

Why did God let this happen to me? What if God didn't? What if we did it to ourselves? What if there's another way? A way to stop thinking in just 'me' terms.

Movement Five:
Our Lonely Conversations with Ourselves

"Sometimes I hear voices in my head, my heart, and in my very soul.

I don't mean real voices, those voices that you hear when you think you're going crazy.

But voices, nonetheless. Sometimes they come from me . . . . Sometimes from others.

It's like an ongoing conversation. Like thinking out loud in high def."

With my TV, with the billboards on the way to work, with my neighbors, with my place of worship, even. Yep, even there.

With my boss, my friends, my enemies, my children, my spouse, my mother or father. My brother-in-law. The one that never quits talking at me.

Now, the conversations do vary a bit. But they tend to ring a common theme:

"Do more, be more, earn more, buy more.

Look better, feel better, live better, die better.

Wear better things, eat better food, drink better beer, travel better places, make better friends, and get a better job for goodness sakes."

I wasn't feeling so lonely on this path until I realized that I shouldn't love myself.

Until I realized that I wasn't beautiful, or smart, or shapely, or thin . . . enough. Enough.

Until I started judging myself. Because I thought others did.

Until I started rejecting myself. Because I thought that I should.

And re-making myself into a self that other 'selves' could love me for.

And listening to the voices of those other selves and myself to myself.

And thinking that, if I can only be a better self in their eyes, I will have made it.

But I never could in the end. And I suffer for it. Why did God let this happen to me?

What if God didn't? What if we did it to ourselves? What if there's another way?

Movement Six:
Our Lonely Conversations with our Faith

I'm a person of strong faith: in the love and grace of God. Mine is a Christian faith tradition. Perhaps yours is the same, perhaps different. Either way is just fine.

Sometimes, faith is hard, though. For many reasons, especially when we're suffering.

It shouldn't be so, but it can be. Sometimes, rigid faith-based rules get in the way.

Dualistic theories get in the way: about good *or* bad; right *or* wrong; body *or* soul; saved *or* not; heaven *or* hell; living goodly *or* badly; righteousness *or* sinfulness; light *or* darkness. "It's gotta be one way *or* the other. Nothing in between. Period!"

Our needless, petty quarrels between faiths also get in the way. Inconsistencies in our teachings get in the way. So do confusing theologies. Yeah, they get in the way.

In some faith circles, discrimination gets in the way. You remember, the Eve thing. "It was *her* fault back in the garden. Let's tip our glasses to patriarchy. And that goes for you too, gay people. You're wrong, too. Get out of the way." And narrow-minded intolerance gets in the way. "You're all little *children* in the faith. We'll tell you what you should believe. Questions welcomed . . . . Sort of. Only one per customer, please."

And let's not forget—"You better get *right* with God, right now. Get on the boat. Straighten up and fly right . . . or you're going to that really bad place when you die . . . . forever. Limited seating for the good place. Have a good eternity."

Oh, and forgive me for almost leaving this one out—"Let's not let too many voices be heard, especially the ones of persons of color, the poor, the marginalized, and those outside the 'acceptable' geographic mainstream of being or thinking or living."

It didn't seem so lonely on this path of faith until I got sick. Until I was suffering.

But what if we actually did this to ourselves? What if there's another way?

Movement Seven:
Another Way—Read with Another Lens

In my Christian faith tradition, I look to the Bible as my primary source.

I love this book and read it daily.

It guides me, grounds me, inspires me, educates me, speaks to me, and challenges me.

Perhaps your faith tradition uses other books. That's great.

But what if we read our religious books with a different lens?

What if we read the Bible as a story, in fact, a series of stories? Jesus taught in parables. He used allegories. It was good enough for him, already . . .

And what if we gave God a break here, and allowed for the Bible's human authorship?

I'm talking about *our* powerful story of mutual seeking. God to us. Us to God. Our 'take' on God's work in our lives. In our very history. Our very souls.

And what if we allowed the Spirit to have guided human hands, minds, and hearts in writing it? Not the dictation or hearing voices thing. But inspiration. Motivation.

Energy, breath, focus, creativity at the heart level. Our heart level.

And what if we got off the literal bandwagon and allowed the Bible to be only broadly historical? Not exactly how it really happened? Perhaps not *all* the details. Rather, interpreted with diverse human contexts, agendas, cultures, and legends? No problem.

Wow, all that would allow the Bible to be ever fresh—continually infused with new meaning. You know, from the Spirit. Like the flow of sparkling, cool water.

It would allow the Bible to better meet us where we are. Exactly where we are.

Right here. Right now. To draw life from it right in the wheelhouse of our suffering.

Without fear of getting a verse wrong. Or forgetting the page. Or violating a rule.

It would still be true. Because God spoke to us through it and still does. Comforting . . .

Movement Eight:
Another Way—Look Elsewhere as Well

So, we have our Bible or other religious book at our bedside. Enough. Right?

"Yep, that's right. That's all we need. Got the Good Book in hand. Done deal."

But stop and think a minute. What if we looked elsewhere, as well?

God spoke with and to the earth when God created this place. And God spoke to people before the Bible was ever penned. So, why should God stop then . . . or even now?

God isn't on a limited talk and text plan. Nope. God's got unlimited minutes and data.

So, what if we tried another way—looking beyond only 'The Book' for God's voice?

You know, to a more diverse and inclusive source of this voice. One who speaks through the Spirit, all creation life, other faith traditions, theology, the voices of those 'left behind', other people, our experiences, our encounters, our reflections, our prayers?

And here's another thought. God isn't just talking. God is listening, too. Actively.

God is asking *us* things. You know, real things. What's our answer? God wants to hear.

And what if God is communicating with us, not just as individuals . . . . but as whole communities? Of whole societies? What are our collective answers?

What if good ideas, good reflections, good answers, and good questions were all around us? Not just in the Good Book. But by using God's 'global' social media platform.

What if God wants us to keep searching, keep moving, keep reading, keep talking, keep watching everywhere? You know, God's wireless network. No lost connections. Never.

And in all of this, we might keep living and acting and loving, then reading and looking and listening some more, then reflecting and questioning, then living and loving some more? Then repeat the cycle. In God's virtual library. The one with parking everywhere. Accessible to all. No card needed to check out the 'books'.

Movement Nine:
Another Way—Walk in Their Boots

Ask yourself this: In whose shoes or boots or sandals are you walking this path of suffering? Are you the only one who's moving at the moment?

If so, you might be looking at *you* as your only reference point. Where are *you* right now? Where are *you* going? How are *you* feeling about it? How are *you*?

What are *your* values, your assumptions, your beliefs, your biases, your fears, your hopes, your wishes, your concerns, and your needs?

You're entitled. You've been through a lot and are still going through it. That's right. Right? Well, you can be entitled to *you*, if that's what you want. You've earned the right. But what if there's another way?

What if you dislocated yourself? What if you 'walked' your suffering today in the shoes of another? What if you tried to see things through his or her eyes and ears and head and heart? Saw everything. Including you.

And what if you more actively took another's point of view about what was going on? Played their part in the story or movement? *Theirs*.

What if you took your suffering to another location, setting, town, part of town, or place for the afternoon or the day or the week? Looked at your pain with the lens of another context: the subway, the city streets, the lake, the ocean, the countryside, the desert, the mountains, the forest, or the stream.

Would any or all of these things take away your suffering? No, they would not.

But they might ease your pain and loss a bit knowing that you're not alone.

They might 'gift' you a different perspective, a new set of eyes in that movement.

For you are special and loved, to be sure. But there's more to you than only you.

Post-Movement Reflection Questions

In what ways has my suffering begun to (or continued to) define me as a person? Why and with what impact?

How have things external to me helped to actually create or exacerbate some of my own suffering? In what ways do I continue to listen to these voices? With what impact?

What guilt do I carry deepest in my heart? Is it truly valid? How does that guilt contribute to my suffering right now?

In what new places can I look for God's peace and presence in my life?

What new lens can I use today for the first time to see the world differently and in a healthier way for me?

Post Movement Rest and Prayer

Loving God, I thank you for creating me as a special, unconditionally loved being. A being in your likeness and image. Created to be included, embraced, and loved. And to love others, in turn. Lord, help me break free from those things that cut me off from myself, from others, and from your world. Help me to say 'no' to things that degrade my inherent worthiness or define me as a person by my pain, suffering, or loss. Assist me in my efforts to see my true value in the goodness of my heart, not in what I acquire, achieve, attain, or possess. With your guiding hand, might I look more broadly at the 'words' that you speak. Words that shower grace and life throughout this world. Might I see your face in all things, not just in books. I pray for those who suffer, not just from disease or loss—but also those excluded from your family for *any* reason. May we all work together to make our faiths more inclusive, loving, and supportive. Especially those who live with pain and sorrow, such as me. In all things, God, might I work to re-connect with life as you intended. Life lived in love, forgiveness, sharing, and caring. Life lived with others. Seen in the way that you see them. Loved in the way that you love them. Embraced in the way that you embrace them. Life lived with you and in you, God. Thank you.

Chapter Four

Where is the Divine in my Suffering?

"Love is as simple as the absence of self given to another. God, when invited, fills the void of any unrequited love; hence loving is how one is drawn closer to God no matter the horrific repercussions."

—CRISS JAMI

Pre-Movement Stretch

When we suffer, we may look to something or someone more powerful than us. To help deal with it. With the pain. With the loss. With the sorrow. With the burden of it all. We look to someone to help carry the load. Help us heal. Help transform. Help make it all go away. Sometimes we look to others for this. Family, friends, neighbors, church members. Sometimes to doctors, nurses, counselors. And sometimes we look to God. But sometimes that's hard to do. In the pages ahead, we'll look at possible reasons why. Why the ways that we describe, define, and look to God may be hurting us more than helping. Using my own Christian faith as a possible framework, we'll look at new ways to vision God, Christ, and the Spirit. We'll explore potentially healthier images of God as life, as a co-suffering presence, and as partial to the poor and suffering. We'll discuss Christ as really human, not just divine. As the rejected one, who understands our own human pain. As sacrificing, not sacrificed for us. And as the bearer of true hope. Finally, we'll explore the Holy Spirit. And look at Spirit as bringer of God's time, as connector, as healer, and as the source of our ever-burning 'pilot light'. My hope is that we'll break some new ground for some. And bring new, more helpful, and affirming ways of thinking about the 'higher power' that we call on when we suffer. A God we can truly love. And who loves us back.

Movement One:
Tidal Wave—Tidal Marsh

The old man awoke from a deep sleep beneath a towering palm tree. He turned over on the cool sand beneath his body. From his back onto his left side. Perhaps he might lie there for a few minutes more before he resumed his walk. The sun was coming up over the horizon. Yet, it was still just dark enough to see the silhouette of the water against the horizon. The wind was blowing harder today, and the man noticed sand on his clothes. The clothes were also damp, covered lightly with the midst of the waves that crashed before him some twenty feet away. The tide was going out. The old man could see the shiny, smooth beach where water lay only hours ago. Seaweed and some driftwood lay on the shore, washed up in the night, he supposed.

The old man marveled at the size of the waves. He wondered at the thunderous sound of their descending crash onto the water's surface as they curled and fell. The great waves churned and frothed as they moved decisively toward the beach. Then, in the span of only seconds, they retreated quickly but meekly away, leaving only the speckles of now-wet grains of sand. The drum and cymbal of each new wave lifted to a grand and nearly deafening crescendo, only to return to the sea in relative quietude. The stark and wondrous cycle then repeated. Each was different. Yet each was the same.

The old man lay nearly in a trance, hypnotized by the power and majesty of the churning sea before him. He didn't notice a stranger who was now sitting beside him. The stranger also stared for some time, engaged in the dramatic action of the teeming waters. She turned to the old man and said, "Quite a show, isn't it? What majesty, what power. It's so inviting, to be a part of those waves. They beckon you to join in and to ride with them." The old man replied, "But you have to respect them. If you're not careful, they can carry you away. The sea is beautiful but also mysterious, powerful, and unforgiving if you misjudge it."

The stranger helped the old man to his feet and invited him to follow her to an area to their right. They walked for a few minutes away from the oceanfront. There, before them, rested a marsh. Trees and scrubs rimmed its perimeters. Tall grass grew from the water below. Lilly pads dotted the quiet tops of this placid pond. The cover of bordering mounds of sand quieted the heavy, surrounding breeze. Birds sang as they darted joyfully from branch to branch. Life sprang from the clear waters of the shallow, protected inlet. The stranger turned to the old man and offered, "You see, this too is also part of the ocean. This tidal marsh is part of the great sea that we watched only a moment ago. It's the same, but it is different at the same time. It's quieter but no less full of voice. It's less majestic but no less powerful. It moves more slowly, but it moves with equal purpose. It doesn't demand our attention, but it is still right here—before us. It doesn't churn its life in its wake. Rather, its stillness gives life room to simply be. It doesn't move as fast as the waves, but it still changes continuously. It doesn't tower before us, but it still amazes. It brings me peace."

The old man looked a final time at the tidal marsh. He thought it was a nice place to simply sit and rest. He felt better having seen this spot today. I'm not as lonely, he thought, as he marveled at the diverse life, which teemed in the gentle waters before him. The man smiled at the stranger and thanked her for this new discovery.

Then the old man shook the stranger's hand and said, "I need to keep moving. I'm seeking the end of the island, where I'll find the answer to my suffering in this life. Time is short and I need to keep moving. But I might come back here on my way home. It's brought me a sense of newfound peace, just like you said. Thank you." The man turned toward the path and began his walk anew.

Movement Two:
God is a Noun

God is a noun. God is a somebody. God is a person.

Not a thing or a being or a member or an 'it'. But a person. A real live person.

But here's the rub. We can't paint a picture of God. We can't even draw God.

We can't take a 'selfie' with God on our phone. With or without our long selfie-stick.

We simply can't. No matter how hard we try. Some person, huh?

We can't even agree on God's name. We call God different things. As if we could give God a proper title? Perhaps, we shouldn't name God at all? No name. No picture.

And then there's the gender thing. Most of us call this person God by a male name.

Well, he's a man, of course. He's our Father. We pray to a 'him'. We say, "Thank you, Father, please Father, forgive me Father, hear our prayer, Father." Him. He.

But is it really true? So, we have a person we can't draw. That we're not sure if 'he's' really a 'he'. With no single name. That we can't really describe at all.

Therein lies one of our problems with God.

God is not us. We are not God. God is 'other'. God defies our efforts to control.

God is mysterious. Defies our efforts to reign in.

Different for different cultures and faiths. Defies our efforts to make God only 'ours'.

And sometimes, God is silent. Or, at least appears to be.

God can seem distant, far off, far away, removed, watching over someone else right now.

Especially when we're suffering or in pain or in grief.

Just when I need God most, I'm the most confused about God.

Just when I need to wrap my arms around something really concrete and real . . .

I sit bewildered. I feel lost. I'm confused about God as a noun.

Movement Three:
God is a Verb

So it's hard to name God as a person, as a noun. Confusing, actually . . .

So, let's look at God as a verb instead. Let's talk about what God 'does'.

God is the creator of all things.

God is a designer, artist, builder, craftsperson, welder, sculptor, architect, surgeon, fitter, plumber, and construction wonder-worker.

God is also the source of all things.

God is the alpha, the beginning, the meaning, the purpose, the core, the fiber. God is the wheel that set all things in motion. You know, got it all started and such.

So, we all got started by God. And we're, therefore, all of God but we are not God. God made us, but is not 'us'. Not we. Not him or her. Not me. Confused?

And therein lies one of our problems with God.

God is transcendent. That means that God was here before us. God will be here after us. For all times, for all places, for all things. Always. Forever. Beyond just us and us.

And because God is not us but has 'done' for us, God also seems to judge us. "I made this place. I make it all work. I look down on it all. I judge it." From the outside.

From above. From the sky. From the clouds.

From the galaxies and the entire universe.

From Heaven itself. And that one hurts the most. That's where I'm trying to get into.

After I'm gone . . . from here . . . from the inside of this place.

Especially when I'm suffering and in pain and grieving. And looking for relief.

I can't name God. I can't even control a self-controlled, transcendent God.

Who sits up there . . . when I'm down here . . . and I'm feeling down. Really down.

Movement Four:
God is an Adjective

So, we're having trouble naming God and describing what God does. A noun is problematic. A verb is problematic. I am problematic. And I'm suffering.

This isn't working. We gotta try something else.

Let's describe God, then. Using adjectives. That's bound to help here.

Here we go then. Think of an adjective. Descriptive. God is loving.

If God is love, then God is *loving*. A kind, caring kind of God.

God loves me, all others, all the animals, the plants, the flowers, all created things.

God loves all people and all things unconditionally. That means that God never waivers. Never. Ever. No siree.

Not one bit. Not for a second. With absolutely no hesitation. Unwavering.

And . . . God is *powerful*. Really, really powerful.

Completely. Totally. To the max. God's got it covered. It's all in God's power. It's all in God's capable, loving, and mighty hands. God will see to it.

And . . . God is *just*.

God wants what's right for us. God wants fairness and justice. God is on our side.

And why not? God created us in the first place.

And therein lies one of our problems with God, especially when we suffer.

If God is loving and powerful and just, why did my sickness just return? Why did the little child get hit by the car? Why did God take my husband of fifty years?

What did he do, she do, I do to make God mad? It makes no sense. None.

So, God can't be all these things: Loving and powerful and just. *And* . . . just let me suffer.

Something's got to give here. I'm suffering. I'm down here and feeling down.

Movement Five:
God in the Past Tense

So, God is hard to describe. And I don't understand how God works. And I'm having a really, really difficult time balancing all of my attributes for God. They don't all add up.

And, on top of that, I'm lonely, sad, in pain, grieving, and at a loss for someone . . .

If not God, what then? Hey, maybe God is dead.

Or never really was. Like all made up. A fabrication.

Or maybe God got everything started nicely and took a hike a while ago. Maybe God said, "Got this all wrapped up after only six days. It's been a long week. I need an extended break. A sabbatical. A vacation. Get off the grid for a while. See ya.

Besides, those humans I created have it all covered. They'll figure it out.

I've given them plenty of talent, grit, determination, wisdom, and direction.

I've given them a big heart. I've written them verses and books. Covered all the religions, I think. And I've sent prophets and saviors. Oh, and I also sent the Spirit, too.

That should do. Besides, they're all mortal. The next generation will make it better.

Looks like I've got this earth thing on cruise control. Call me if you need me."

And therein lies one of our problems with God.

Many of us simply quit calling God. God didn't take a hike. Maybe we did . . .

We look to books, to experts, to scribes, to the web, to our smart phones, to our social media accounts, to the celestial stars, to the movie stars, to the pundits, to the wiz-kids.

We look to our children, our parents, our universe, our neighbors, our adversaries, and ourselves. Yeah, a lot to ourselves. Until we start suffering. Until we really hurt.

Until we're stuck down here and we're feeling abandoned and down.

Really alone. Really down. And God feels truly 'gones-ville'.

Movement Six:
Another Way—God as Powerful Love

What if God was Love? Not just love, but a *powerful* love? What if the power of God's love truly defined the 'who, what, and why' of God?

The kind of love that wants the best, the fullest, the most loving, liberated life for us . . .

Not a jealous, possessive, obsessive, compulsive, and destructive kind of love.

Not the kind of love that makes otherwise well meaning people say:

"Sorry for your loss, William. I guess that God needed another angel in heaven."

"Sorry about his passing, Mary. But heaven is a little better place now with Ted there."

"Sorry about your loss, Joe. I guess God loved your best friend too much."

"Sorry about your pain, Sue. But God never gives you more than you can handle."

"Sorry about this situation, Pete. God must really be angry with you. What did you do?"

No, not that kind of love. But an unconditional, non-stop, grace-filled love for us. That's right. For us. Powerful. Powerfully present and loving. Power-packed.

I'm talking about the kind of love where God sits with you in your sorrow and pain and grief. The kind of love that brings loving people to your side when you hurt. The kind of love that powers you to go on . . . sometimes to simply go on. To be open to tomorrow. The kind of love that brings unexpected blessings in pain's midst. The kind of love that brings unexpected hope. The kind of love that brings a new friend into your grieving space. The kind of love that slowly brings a smile to your face when you remember someone lost. A smile that walks with your tears. Perhaps a smile before the tears for a change. A loving, happy memory. A new memory. A fresh memory coming back.

That's a powerful love. It's there. God is there in the thick of things. Quietly transforming, healing, sustaining, comforting you with all God's power. *If* we let God.

Movement Seven:
Another Way—God as Just Life

God is a God of life, not death.

Why in the world would God create us only to destroy us? Please explain this to me.

What kind of God relishes death, poverty, marginalization, destruction, starvation, disease and sickness, grief, and sorrow? And suffering, for Pete's sake.

What if all the stories about God's wrath were simply ours . . . about God? You know, my enemy has been vanquished. "Thanks, God. It must have been *you* doing it. Good stuff.

Things really worked out. They got what was coming to them. Must have been you, God. There's no other explanation. Good deal. Way to put them down, God. I need to bookmark this one for posterity. That's the way that I saw it." Our dream. Not God's.

And here's another story of ours: The whole God kicking us out of the Garden of Eden in the Bible. You know, in a rage, where God condemns us to 'ashes' in the end? Because we ate from the fruit of the tree of knowledge. Because we were bad. Is that God's story or ours? Maybe one we made up about God? Not God's story about us.

So, what if God actually sent us out from the Garden on purpose? With a real purpose.

What if God wants us to journey, to live, and to love? In peace.

In 'just' harmony and community. Where everyone is welcome.

In all life's fullness. Now, that's a good story. God's. Not ours.

What if God's life in us is a light, sometimes flickering, sometimes burning brightly?

What if *our* job is to keep the light burning? To make it burn more brightly. To share it with others in peace, harmony, community, fullness . . . and love.

What if that light is our compass, our guide, our true self, the very meaning of our lives?

I mean life. A God-filled life. A just and interdependent life. I mean real life.

Movement Eight:
Another Way—God as Co-Sufferer

In my Christian heritage, we hear it all the time. God sent God's Son to die on the cross. That's why Jesus came. To save us. There, on the Cross. In fact, we say it:

"God punished God's son in our place. We had it coming. But Jesus took our place."

Or . . . "God sacrificed God's son in an epic battle with Satan. The devil still exists, but the outcome is now ensured. Satan is a 'gonner' in the end. Thanks, God."

We're covered now. We're forgiven. All is OK. Sorry about that, Jesus.

But that makes God a child abuser. Something evil. Something unloving.

I don't think so. Not the God that I know, anyway . . .

What if Jesus died on the cross because of *us*? What if *we* killed God in God's own name? Because Christ scared some powerful people with his teaching and healing.

Because Jesus was different. He was prophetic. He was challenging. He was disruptive.

What if God didn't cause Christ's death at all?

But allowed it to happen because God's grace and love matter most of all.

Because violence, retribution, and a showy kind of power wasn't God's thing.

And what if God actually joined in Christ's forsakenness on the cross? Yes, joined.

Grieved this loss. Felt Christ's pain. Didn't die, but died inside a lot.

Like any parent who loses a child. A crushing pain and loss. By God. At the Cross.

Like someone just punched you in the stomach and you can't breath. Gasping for air.

Then feeling the utter, deafening silence of Christ's death. Then didn't walk away from us. But forgave humanity's greatest possible crime. To show us true love. Then suffered with us in this. With grace and love. Yep, God. For us.

Then resurrected Christ so that love won in the end. Yep, God. For us.

Movement Nine:
Another Way—God as Partial to the Poor

"Molly must be living right with God. She's made it big in the stock market. She has a new job, a new car, and a big new house in the burbs. And another place at the shore. With a boat, no less. She has her health, her family, and her money. Wow, she must be living right. Doing it all the right way. She's good with God, for sure. "

"Poor Betty. She struggles to make ends meet. Lives paycheck-to-paycheck. Never enough to get by on, I'm afraid. Struggles with her children. One's a drug addict. The other's usually in trouble for other stuff. Those kids never made anything of themselves. Betty really suffers. I wonder what went wrong with her? You think God is angry?"

Sure, God takes care of God's own. You know, the ones who've lived right, prayed right, and most of all: made something of themselves. Made it. They are now Made.

But what if making it, spending it, living it up, buying it, enjoying it, or giving it all away has nothing to do with God's favor?

What if God is partial not to the rich, but to the poor and the suffering? Yes, them.

Not because God likes them better.

Or because they're more worthy. Or without fault.

But because God wants us *all* to have life in all its fullness.

God doesn't want anyone left behind, marginalized, forgotten, suffering, and in pain.

Any kind of pain. Any kind of loss.

So, maybe suffering isn't God's punishment at all.

But an aberration of God's hope and loving plan for us. For All of us.

And what if God looks with special favor on those who suffer?

Because they suffer. Because God knows that suffering's not right.

Movement Ten:
Another Way—We are Of and In God

"So, you're telling me that God is present, especially for those who suffer.

Powerful, but in a different kind of way. Grace-filled and ever loving.

But, I'm suffering and in pain. And God feels pretty silent at the moment.

Crickets, really. I'm waiting. And I'm waiting. What gives, God? Where are you?"

Sometimes God does feel absent. But here's a thought: We can't long for something that's not already in us. Here for us. Greater than us. Forever for us.

How can we love God and others if someone didn't put that in our hearts to start with?

Someone who loved us first. Yes, us.

How can we grieve our loneliness and isolation if someone didn't create us to live with others in love . . . in the first place? Yes, us.

How can we marvel at the sheer wonder of creation if that's something that we humans cooked up? Yeah, tossed it together a few years back. Like a picnic lunch or something.

No. We look with amazement at the stars in the sky. Towering peaks. Turquoise, clear oceans. Majestic waterfalls. The effortless gallop of a beautiful horse.

Nothing ho-hum about that. Not a tossed salad here. No. It's a brilliant buffet.

And we didn't do it. God did it. Then God gave it to us to care for.

God is not 'us' and is not those things. But God is *in* us and *in* those things.

And we're in God's image and likeness because God loved us and made us first.

God invites us to live for the God who made us and loves us. Even when we suffer.

Especially when we suffer. Because we're not alone.

Even when God seems distant and far away. Even then, God is near.

Even then, we're with God. That's comforting when we suffer. Especially then.

Movement Eleven:
Jesus as Divine Savior and King

In my faith tradition, Jesus is Savior and King.

Jesus came, Jesus died, Jesus rose. We are saved. A neat, tidy equation.

In some cases, we talk mostly about the conception part, the passion on the cross part, and the rising part. Those are the important things, aren't they?

We tend to leave a lot out of the actual living part.

The part about Christ here with us in the flesh.

Now, to be fair, it's hard. The Biblical Gospels are not an autobiography. Jesus didn't leave us anything he penned. He was busy with other things. Not a writer, I'm afraid.

In fact, the Gospels are not even true biographies. A whole bunch is missing about Jesus.

And there's not just one story. Four guys got into the writing act here. And they're different to a point. Now it's getting complicated.

So, what we're taught is that Jesus came for us, he died for us, and he rose for us. Along the way, he performed miracles. Lots and lots of them.

Like feeding thousands from next to nothing. Like casting out the demons. Like curing people. Like bringing back the dead. Not the ordinary stuff of everyday human labor.

Pretty flashy deeds, to be sure. Jesus was Divine. Remember that.

Now granted, he was also human. Pause . . . "But we need to focus on the Immaculate Conception. The virgin birth. The turning water into wine. The miracle healings. And waking the dead. Let's stay on task here. And remember that, after his passion on the cross, he rose from the dead. Jesus appeared to many of his followers. Then he headed up to heaven. He actually rose. Yep, Divine. The stuff of celestial, kingly power. You know, Other. Remember that."

Movement Twelve:
Another Way—Jesus as Human Too

"Jesus came from above. Stuck around for a while. Then headed back to heaven.

He was human, kind of. Just for a while. Probably just for show. Mostly divine.

Heck, maybe Christ didn't even really die on the cross.

Maybe it was a divine slight of hand. Maybe Jesus just appeared to be human.

Trick's on you, silly people down there."

But what if Jesus really was human? Not just divine. Really, really human too.

Wow. That means that he actually ate, slept, rubbed his eyes in the morning, washed his face, got thirsty, yawned, scratched his head.

Got headaches, got stomachaches, got seasick, got tired, and maybe even got cranky.

Wait for it . . . . And actually went to the bathroom.

We rarely talk about what it might be like to actually have *lived* being Jesus.

What it was like to laugh, to cough, to cry, to sing, and maybe to even snore like Jesus.

What it was like to fear, to dance, to shout, to shudder, and to bow one's head like Jesus.

What it was like to grow up, to play, to learn, to develop, and to mature like Jesus.

And what if he did all those things? Even the bathroom part.

Would he be any less our Christ?

Jesus was Divine. But he was also Human.

The real thing. In the flesh. Not the bad flesh of the Garden, as we've been taught.

But flesh nonetheless.

Why do we have trouble with that? Jesus came for us, not just to save us.

But to actually *be* with us. It's hard to show us God's image and plan without actually doing the actual person thing. Especially for those who suffer. What if that's all right?

Movement Thirteen:
Another Way—Jesus as Rejected

"OK. So Jesus was actually human, not just divine. I'll reluctantly buy that.

But he was King. Our Savior. The Anointed One. He was the founder of the Christian faith. We praise him, we worship him, we glorify him, and we build giant cathedrals for him. We kneel before him. We light candles for him. We paint him. We sculpt him.

King. Savior. King. Born to be King. Sure thing."

But what if Christ didn't come as King? What if he wasn't born to be King? Didn't even want to be King? Not even a little bit.

Christ was born in a cave. Not into wealth, either. His father was a simple man. His mother was a simple woman. They probably just 'got by' financially. No second home.

Oh, and Jesus was a Jew. He was a Galilean Jew. Part of a people rejected by the powerful as backwards, half-breeds, and illiterates.

Not particularly welcome if you know what I mean.

Oh, and Jesus was homeless of sorts in his later life. You know, really homeless. The kind of people who many of us look down on. Admit it. Come on. Admit it.

Oh, and he was inclusive. Brought along tax collectors, prostitutes, women, the poor, and others who were marginalized. He didn't hang out with the in-crowd . . . the clique. Oh, and he drank with these 'losers'. Wine. Not grape juice. The high-octane stuff.

Oh, and he rejected power, force, empty ritual, oppression, and hypocrisy. In your face.

Oh, and he proclaimed a pretty radical idea: the Reign of God. Ah, a prophet too.

In other words, he lived 'on the margins'. Out there. Rejected and poor.

Like we feel when we suffer. So, maybe Jesus actually understands what we're going through. He lived it too. As a human, not just some divine guy.

Movement Fourteen:
Another Way—Jesus as Sacrificing, Not Sacrificed

The cross. The old, rugged cross. Where Christ hung. On the cross.

Maybe Christ never saw it coming until the days right before the end.

Maybe he did. And still faced it anyway. The cross . . .

Who would blame him if he tried to sidestep that one? What an awful way to die.

The Romans liked the cross back then. Good for revolutionaries, scoundrels, dirt bags.

Great way to keep things orderly, tidy, and peaceful. With brute force and fear.

Good for punishing the worst of the worst. In the worst, most gruesome and painful way.

Kill them slowly. Then leave them up there to be eaten by the vultures.

Or take them down and leave them there, dead. To be eaten by dogs and wolves.

What if Christ saw it coming because he lived on the margins? Did things that scared the powerful, challenged everything, turned over tables, got others mad.

And kept doing what he was doing. Because he was about a different way.

And he faced it and shouldered it and died on it, even though he could have avoided it.

Or powered through it. Or made a miracle and made it go away.

What if Christ bore it and sacrificed himself? Because responding in love was a better way? Because he knew that hate would not win the day.

Nor would power. Neither, ultimately.

Nor would a magic disappearing act. "Now you see him, now you don't. Hey, wait a minute. Where did he go?" Nope, he didn't go. He stayed. And died right there.

Because it was important to love us and suffer with us in our time of greatest darkness and emptiness. When we deserved it least of all . . . Christ stayed for us through it all.

Movement Fifteen:
Another Way—The Resurrection Hope

What if the most important thing isn't that Christ suffered and died?

But that Christ forgave us right there on the cross before he died?

That God chose *not* to walk away from humanity . . .

When humanity deserved it most? Yes, us. At our worst.

What if God's non-violent love mattered most on that Friday we call 'Good'? Was more powerful and mighty. Than ever before or after.

And what about the next day? Saturday.

The day that we 'cruise' right past between Good Friday and Easter Sunday. That day.

When the disciples grieved and cried. When they were disheartened and frankly scared to death. When everything seemed most empty for Christ's followers after the cross.

When maybe they thought they'd been betrayed. "Like, maybe we were . . . wrong . . . about this guy. Dead wrong. Totally. He's toast. We're toast."

When they wondered where do we go now? What's next? Are we next on the cross?

But that Saturday wasn't the end, after all. "Keep reading, everyone. Keep the faith. Don't leave me just yet. Stay tuned. Turn the channel NOW."

Taaaa daaa. Sunday. Christ was raised. A victory for the little people. A clear message.

Suffering and pain and death and loss were not the final words. Hope and life are.

Sometimes it just seems like the other way. But, it's not really the way.

Because life lived, after all. Hope lived after all. Love lived after all. God won.

That's especially important to remember when we suffer and grieve in our pain.

To remember that God did not place us on our cross. And God will not leave us there, either. God takes us down and brings us to God's love. If only we want it.

Movement Sixteen:
The Spirit as Our Doer

In my religious tradition, we call it the Holy Trinity.

'Father, Son, and Holy Spirit'. The Big Three.

Three in one. One in three. Once or so each year at church, we try to explain the Trinity.

We use lots and lots and lots of analogies. I'm not sure whether they help or not.

But, in fact, we generally forget the third person. You know, the Spirit. The third one.

Now, to be fair, many of us say "In the name of the Father, Son, and Holy Spirit." Many of us also repeat a creed every Sunday when we say a few words about the Spirit.

But that's about it. "If we can't explain it, let's not dwell on it. OK?"

Admittedly, some churches talk a lot about the Holy Spirit. Some believe that the Spirit *is* in the church. 'Our' church. 'Our' Spirit. Staying at 'Our' place.

Within our four walls. Under our steeple. There. Powering us and our sacraments. Ours.

Next, others believe that Jesus gave us the Spirit after he died and before he rose. On the holy day we call Pentecost. Once and for all.

Drum roll. Big moment. Then and there. Not a second before.

Like the Spirit wasn't there from the very beginning. It's a Christian thing. Ours.

Finally, lots of us also call on the Spirit. Regularly. When we need something.

"Come Holy Spirit. Right now, please. I really need you to do this. Or that."

"Ahhh, the good old work-horse Spirit. Dependable. Just a call away. Ours."

So, the Holy Spirit is a Christian thing, within the church, in the sacraments, and always doing. That's that. Got it. But what about everyone and everything else? Hmmm . . .

Especially when we suffer. Especially when we don't go to any church.

Especially when we're alone and gasping and need help . . . being and breathing.

Movement Seventeen:
Another Way—Spirit as Time Machine

Tick . . . Tick . . . Tick.

Time is always moving. Past-to-present-to-future.

Nice and neat. Linear. From there-to-here-to-there. And then to the next thing. Next.

Can't be late. Just in time. Not a second too soon. In a split second. Prompt.

Progressing normally. Right on schedule. Until. Until I got sick. Until my sister died. Until I lost my best friend. Until my grieving and pain and suffering began.

Then time, as I knew it, stopped. Got all mixed up. The past now keeps haunting my present. My future is unclear. In fact, I may have no future. And today stinks, too. Bad.

But what if God's 'time' isn't ours? What if the Spirit helps to bridge us to God's time?

What if Spirit helps to think about time differently? Helps us not to forget the happier times in the past. Supports us with those memories. The *yesterdays* that strengthen us.

And helps us to put troubling yesterdays behind us. Move on a little. From yesterday.

And comes into our hearts to help us make *today* a little more meaningful and manageable. And flexible. Open to another way, another option, alternative, or plan.

And enters into us to help us to think differently about *tomorrow*.

Even when tomorrow doesn't look so promising. Even when we want to quit.

Keeping us open to the possibilities. To a new future. Not the same, but different.

Where we can honor and remember the past, work through today, and walk a little further. Toward tomorrow. With a little more peace and hope.

Even if tomorrow has been changed forever.

What if there's another way? A way where the Spirit changes *our* notion of time. What if Spirit brings us into God's time? More fully into God's love. Always on time.

Movement Eighteen:
Another Way—Spirit as Connector

"So, I'm having a really lousy day. Just wanted you to know that.

No one understands what I'm going through right now.

If one more person says, 'I understand', my head's going to explode. I know they mean well, but they don't really understand. Not At All. Because they're not me.

And frankly, I'm feeling pretty alone right now. No one really gets it. Gets me. Me."

But what if someone really got you? Knew you. Could say 'I understand you'. And really, really understand you. 'You' as a special, unique, and loved person. You.

What if Spirit lived within you and was with you from the very moment of your birth?

I mean from the start. Not when you started to walk. Or to run. Or to ride a bike.

But from the beginning. Before you were even born. Wow. That's early.

And actually breathed your first breath for you—right when you left your mother's womb.

And helps you to breathe right now, when your suffering suffocates your life.

Because the Spirit knows you, loves you, prays for you when you can't, and intercedes for you to God . . . even when you can't figure out what you even want anymore.

Because Spirit knows you and knows God. A Person of the Godhead. The living, loving breath in you. Part of God's family. Part of yours. Yes, yours.

So, Spirit keeps you connected to yourself and to God, even when you feel like a leaky life raft. Even when you feel like you're floating out there without any oars.

Encouraging you and advocating for you with God, who understands your suffering. Because the Spirit connects you. So you're not alone after all. Even when you think you are. Because the Spirit is holding your hands. And holding God's hands.

Together in a circle. Together. Holding hands.

Movement Nineteen:
Another Way—Spirit as Healer

"I'm terribly sorry to give you this news, Ms. Williams. You suffered a severe heart attack. We were able to bring you back. But the prognosis isn't good, I'm afraid."

So, the outlook isn't good. I'm now disabled. I'm limited. I'm constrained. I'm on a timeline. Not my own. But my disease's. My doctor says what I got isn't curable.

That means I'll never be a real person again. Never cured. Never whole.

Never fulfilled. Never healed. Never. Never. So now what?

But what if the Spirit helped us to heal . . . even when we're not 'curable'?

Even when we're limited and constrained. Not full speed.

'Full speed' by our definition. You know, the human one. The one we've made up.

What if Spirit helped us to redefine the word 'healing'? That word. That one.

Helped us to heal as *we* define it. You know, get completely better. Where possible.

But also helped us heal in another way. 'Both-And' here. To a healing that opens us up to God's blessings *even* when we hurt. Yes, even when we hurt.

Opens our heart to others a little more. To their sorrows and pains. Even when we hurt.

Opens our minds to something new, even with our 'limitations'. Even when we hurt.

Opens our souls to love more, even in the face of our setback. Even when we hurt.

Open ourselves to change. Even change we didn't plan for. Even when we hurt.

To a life that can still have meaning and purpose. And fulfillment. And some joy.

Even when the world says that we didn't heal. Not completely. No sir.

But we *did* heal some. Maybe we healed a lot. Even if the world doesn't think so.

What if Spirit helped us heal in *every* way? Even if it's not *our* way right now.

What if Spirit found a way? Perhaps, our way. But also a different way.

Movement Twenty:
Another Way—Spirit as Pilot Light

"Some days, I feel the life literally sucking out of me. Like someone's sitting on my chest. And forcing air out of my lungs. Literally sucking it out. Against my will."

And, if it were OK to say it, I would say, 'This sucks.' But I can't. But it does, really.

And, along with the air sucking out, my life feels like it's seeping out.

My energy is gone. Perhaps, so am I. Maybe I'll be gone soon. Forever.

There's not a lot to live for anymore, I guess.

Why go on? Can someone tell me why I should go on? For what? Really.

Perhaps, a lot of days feel like that. Or worse. Really? Really.

But what if the Spirit didn't give up on you, even when you were ready to?

What if Spirit was like an old friend? Who refused to leave your side. Never. Ever.

Who gave you a reason. A reason to keep trying. To keep living.

Who would not let God's eternal flame in you go out. Not let the light go out.

Not let you go out. Never. Ever.

Who kept the home fire burning. In you. Even when everyone and everything kept splashing cold water on it. And trying to put it out. But it simply wouldn't go out.

Like a pilot light on a stove that could not be extinguished. Never. Ever.

And even if you breathed your last breath here on earth, who kept the home fire burning.

In you. Would not let it go out. Not a chance. Never. Ever.

Because there was a light and flame left. Because God put it there in the first place.

And the Spirit would not let it ever go completely out. Even when you thought it had. You know, when you 'didn't make it'. But, actually, you did.

Because Spirit carried it in love back to God. To go on. Forever. Always.

Post-Movement Reflection Questions

Who and What is the Divine presence or spirit for me?

How is my 'picture' of God helping or hurting me during this time of suffering? How is it bringing me greater or lesser comfort right now?

Which long-standing notion of the Divine do I need to question or re-examine at this time?

How can I begin to see God in a more present, loving, understanding, and grace-filled way in my life?

How can I better allow the Divine Spirit to move into and through me with greater freedom and healing power?

Post-Movement Rest and Prayer

Loving God, knowing you as 'you are' is hard sometimes. Especially when I hurt inside and out. Especially when I'm alone and feel alone. Especially when you feel distant. It's difficult to define you, describe you, and even know how you act at times. I struggle to match up your love, your power, and your just heart with my suffering and loss. I pray that, with your loving presence and guidance, I might come to know your power in new ways. Empowering, loving, supportive, and present ways. Here, now, in my very midst. Might I come to know your love through your own suffering. Through your own sacrifices. Through your own rejection.

Through your own abiding love, especially for the poor and lost. Through your own human presence and model through Jesus. One who lived with us and knows our pain. On a real, human level. I pray that you might heal, transform, give meaning, and love through and in my pain. That your Spirit might help me to live more fully in your 'time', not just my own. That I might forever be connected to you while on this earth. That the light you placed in me at birth might never go out. That it might shine as brightly as possible. Even in my pain and sorrow. In hope, as well. Hope borne in you. Thank you, God.

Chapter Five

Where is my Human Support?

"We must learn to regard people less in the light of what they do or omit to do, and more in the light of what they suffer."

—Dietrich Bonhoeffer

Pre-Movement Stretch

Other than higher powers, we often look most to others right here for help. When we suffer. We look for companionship, help, a listening ear, the gentle touch of a caring hand, the hug or embrace of someone we love. Someone else . . . to walk with us, sit with us, cry with us, to somehow understand us, to join us in our pain. If only for a moment. To share the moment. To share the pain and sorrow. It's only natural. For we weren't made to be alone. To suffer alone. No. We're made for community. For communion. To share time, space, relationship, and love. In the pages ahead, we'll explore the ways in which others might better come along with us when we suffer. Or we with them. Or both. We'll talk about the power of our stories and those of others. About finding common interests and goals in ways that break down barriers. Conversely, we'll delve a bit into the healthy boundaries that we also need. How they help us to be truly 'us', not fused with others in damaging ways. We'll also talk about the difference between 'wants' versus 'needs'. And between being scratched versus clawed. And how to forgive others more readily when our needs aren't met. Or when we're really clawed. We'll explore another crucial difference: between feeling sorry 'for' someone versus feeling 'with' another. Much of that difference lies in the quality of 'connection' that we maintain with others during times of pain, sorrow, and loss. We'll end on the business of 'un-finished business'—why it's important to say the things that most need saying. While we can. While closure is possible. And healthy. And healing. And grace-filled. Helping us to move on, whatever 'on' might mean.

Movement One:
Celestial Companionship

The old man sat quietly at the water's edge. The day's sun had set some hours ago. The sky morphed gently and slowly. First, bright blue. Then, a darker, deeper shade. Then, dimmed as the brilliant sun faded into the horizon. Then darkness. At first, there was simply darkness, as no moon shone. But a cloudless sky gave way to bright, emerging stars. They shone and flickered the slightest beams of light toward the place where the man sat. He scanned the broad expanse of sky for one star, the North Star. He always looked for it. He was drawn to it, like an old metal dish to a magnet. Try as he might otherwise, finding that star was always first. It gave him his grounding. A centering. His place on this planet that he called home.

The old man heard footsteps approaching. By now, he was accustomed to uninvited guests. Perhaps it was good to rest and talk with someone for a few minutes after all tonight. Without the brightness of the moon, he couldn't walk further today in any event. Too dark. He might fall on the path. There was no one there to help him up. Best to simply sit for the night. And have some company for a change. A stranger came alongside the old man, and asked, "Can I sit and join you for awhile? My feet and legs are tired from the day." Before waiting for the old man's response, the stranger sat and continued, "Beautiful sky, tonight. You know, without the moon, the stars shine brighter. It's easier to see them when the sky is darker." The old man replied, "Yes. I like to look at the sky at night. So much more interesting than in the day. There's hardly a cloud in the sky around here. Unless it rains. Not much to look at in the daylight."

The stranger turned toward the old man and asked, "Which star is your favorite?" The old man assuredly answered, "The North Star. I look for it whenever the night skies permit." The stranger looked toward the stars and agreed. He added, "Yes, that's a popular one, for sure. Humans have used it for centuries. It's a practical kind of star. Like a working person. Guides us. Keeps us on track. Keeps us focused on where we're heading, I guess. What other stars do you look for?" The old man thought for a moment. Nothing much came to mind. He thought for a second more, but didn't want to ignore the stranger's question altogether. So, he responded, "None, really. The North Star is the one. I follow that one all year, all the time. I watch it in the sky, but that's the one I like." The stranger pressed on, "What else do you see when you look at it?" The man replied, "I guess some other stars around it."

The stranger pointed to the North Star. He asked the old man to follow his arm as it lifted that way. He appeared to draw a broad circle around the star. And he asked the old man to focus on all the stars within its large radius. "What do you see when you look at all the other stars?" he asked. The man looked perplexed. He asked back, "What do you mean what do I see?" The stranger offered, "What shapes do you see? What things?"

The old man gazed more broadly for a minute. Then he gazed some more. He had never done this before. He thought about something for a second, then dismissed it. The stranger responded, "Don't think about it too much. What do you see when you first look?" The old man replied, "I guess I see a face there. Perhaps an animal's body over here. And out there, I see a strange shape. But I like the face most."

"Yes," said the stranger. We see lots of things. When we look beyond that which we look for first. Each time we look outward from the center of our gaze, we're met with new and different things. It's never the same, really. One night, it's this. Another night, it's that. Kind of interesting, don't you think?" The old man pondered on that one for a second. He added, "Yes, I guess you have a point. I still like the North Star the best, though. It keeps me grounded. It's dependable and sure. It's steady." The stranger returned, "That's fine. Good to be grounded in something. But the North Star stands out most for me because it's surrounded by a lot of other stars. It's like that star has a host of friends who travel with it. Who always help us find our own North Star. Friends who always mark it in the sky each night. The North Star wouldn't be nearly as interesting if it sat out there alone, now would it? And here's something else to think about. What if all those other stars helped to hold the North Star in the sky?"

The old man reflected a bit on that one. But he came back, "Now, we know that stars don't hold other stars up. I don't know why, but I just know it isn't so." The stranger smiled and returned, "Don't be too sure. And even if it's not completely true, they all work better when they're in the sky together." The stranger briefly placed his hand on the old man's shoulder. He gently used it to help himself up. "Good to talk with you tonight. I appreciated the company," the stranger said. The old man reached for the stranger's hand. The old man said, "I could use a hand getting up, myself." They both smiled. The man offered his goodbye and said, "See you down the path, maybe." The stranger replied, "Yes, like the stars. Like the stars."

Movement Two:
The Importance of Community

"I can do this one myself, but thank you."

"If I stop doing things on my own, I'll become too dependent on others."

"If I don't push Ted to take care of these things himself, he'll stop even trying anymore."

"If I can't take care of myself any longer, I'll lose my independence. That matters a lot."

Independence. Self-reliance. Do it yourself. Just do it. You can do it. You.

I take care of myself, look after myself, count on myself, and just do it myself. Myself.

Now, being, laughing, sharing, celebrating, and doing things is just fine *with* others.

Sometimes. When everything is going well. When I feel well. And not needy.

"But when the chips are down, when the rubber meets the road, I need to count on myself. I don't want to be a burden on others. I can't drag them down with me . . . "

But what if we weren't made to do it ourselves? Not made to do it alone.

What if God truly wants us to count on others? Actually lean on them.

And not just to count on them. But to be with them in everything.

Even during the bad stuff. Even when we're suffering. Especially then.

What if we were created to *be* interdependent, not independent? Made to be and live in community? All the time. Not by ourselves.

What if being and living in communion were more important than our little old selves?

For we are constructed as unique, valued individuals, but we matter most as multiples.

What if God is happiest when things and people work together seamlessly?

We're not some individual cogs or parts. We belong to each other. We need each other.

That means that we 'just do it', but do it together.

Even when we suffer.

Movement Three:
The Importance of Story

"So, did you hear the one about the man who walked into a bar . . . ?"

"You'll never guess what Ginny told me about Celine the other day . . . "

"I read this story online today. It was amazing. I couldn't believe that this guy did it."

"Last night's game was a shocker. No way the team could blow it in the second half.

But they did. No way . . . . Actually, way."

We talk a lot about stories. Those we read, see, scan, search for, hear about.

But *we* are stories, too. We. We are many, many things.

But most of all, we *are* our stories.

Stories make up the fabric of our lives. They tell us and others about who we are, where we've been, what we've done, what our children and grandchildren have done, what we've lost . . . who we've lost.

And they tell us what we're facing right now. In the midst of our suffering and pain.

Stories are nouns, verbs, adjectives, and adverbs. They are how we communicate 'us'.

To others. To us. About us, our feelings, our hopes, our fears, and our deepest secrets.

We don't live life in the abstract. But in real time. In story language.

Short stories. Long stories. Text stories. Action stories. Reflective stories.

Stories with lots of pictures. Illustrations. Photos.

Sometimes we write others about our stories. Sometimes we'd rather talk about them.

Sometimes we'd rather not talk about them, but we need to. Especially when we suffer.

Because stories affirm us. Remind us that we are 'somebodies' worth something.

Help us to think back, remember, wonder, question, and ponder our lives.

To make some sense of things. To connect with others. Especially when we hurt.

Movement Four:
While Not Internalizing Others'

So, we all have our stories. They matter.

Because they tell others about us. And us about us. Me about me.

About our place and shape and purpose and meaning in this life. From this life.

And we're meant to share our stories with others.

Because we were made to be with others.

To sit with others and listen to their stories. Help them share these stories more fully.

More honestly, more completely, more transparently.

And, we were made to truly, truly listen to the stories of others. Fully. Not just catching part of it as a pause in telling our own story.

But by actually entering into *their* stories. Engaging with them more deeply. Not on the surface level.

Not the "Yes, that's interesting. Thanks for sharing. But I really have to go. Sorry for leaving so quickly." Then, "Whew. Glad to be out of there. Now onto the next thing."

But, the "I am here for you. I'm here to sit with you. Tell me more about that. I'm really interested. *You* are the most important thing for me today."

Stories matter and help, especially when they're shared and really listened to . . .

As long as we don't 'internalize' the stories of others.

Listening and engaging aren't the same things as internalizing. Not the same thing as owning them. Not assuming the stories of others about myself. Not the same. Their stories are not my story. Their's. Not mine. I don't have to accept them as my own.

Even when the stories say nice things about me. Even when they don't. I can grow from and learn from them. But I don't need to 'become' them.

Movement Five:
Finding Common Interests

"This has really got me in a bind. My family wants me to move into smaller quarters.

They say that I can't take care of myself anymore. They're worried about me.

Like I'll fall and not get up. Lay there. For hours. Suffer alone. Maybe forever.

Who would know? Who would even ask? They're too busy to call me these days.

So, they have a point. But I'm not moving. I want my place. My independence."

We take care of ours. First things first.

For, if we don't watch out for our own interests, then who will?

"That's my opinion on this. I stand by my position. I'm fixed. I'm right. Locked in."

Into my opinion, position, fixed point, locked-in mindset. Mine. Gotta look after myself.

But what if my position in this thing was less important than a better *outcome*?

If I stepped back from the ledge, loosened my grip, took a wider view, and actually talked about goals and outcomes, not means and methods? What might happen?

It's possible that those I disagree with might have the same vision and goals after all. That we see the 'what' the same way, really. We just look at the 'how to go about it' differently. Maybe there's a way to get there together, instead of moving apart.

What if we constructively shared our fears, hopes, concerns, and possibilities? First.

Not our opinions, our options, our plan, and our process. Our way . . . or the highway.

At least not in the beginning. And never about the highway thing.

But focused, instead, on the big picture, not the little ones. First things first.

Actually focused on finding points of agreement about my situation, my limitations, my risks, and my possibilities. Building a common way forward. Together. Aligned.

Driven by our shared interests, not our divided, rigid positions. Driving together.

Movement Six:
Without Violating Boundaries

Sharing is good. Very, very good. Because we love each other.

We share our stuff, our time, our friends, our moments, our joys, our sorrows.

We even share our clothes sometimes. Like my favorite sweater. Like my favorite recipe, my favorite vacation spot, my power tools, a loaf of bread.

"We share everything. That's good, isn't it? You said we're supposed to get together."

So, together is good. But so are fences. Short ones, but fences nonetheless.

The old line rings eternally true: Good fences make good neighbors.

Fences help us to hold 'our' space in this world. They help to keep *out* the stuff that we don't need in our lives. And even limit the things that we do sometimes.

They're boundaries. We need them. Especially when we suffer.

They're violated when others try to break down the fence: fuse their fears, burdens, stories, complaints, anger, and rage into your yard. Or when you try to do the same.

Or when they build the fence higher between your yards. Or you try to do the same.

Because a two inch fence is not a fence at all. And because you can't see over a ten foot tall one. Not even a little.

Good boundaries mean that you help to carry the unfair and unruly burdens of others.

But not their daily loads. They mean that you care deeply about others. You're truly there for them. But you're not taking over their lives or telling them what's best.

Good boundaries mean that you come together in healthy ways. Boundary gamesmanship, power trips, ego roulette, fence jumping, or separation aren't healthy. Nope. Especially when you hurt and suffer. You need others to heal. But you also need good boundaries. To heal. To be you. Because you matter.

Movement Seven:
Being Clear about your Needs

"I want this to all go away. Now. Completely. I'm sick of it. Sick of being sick.

I want a miracle. I want the nurses to quit poking me, sticking me, and waking me up.

In the middle of the night. Throughout the night. All night long.

I want my family to come visit me. I want them to call me. To be worried about me.

I want someone to actually listen to me for a change."

"I have a public announcement to make. Testing, Testing ... 1, 2, 3. Hey, no one is listening to me. Can you hear me? Anyone?"

Sometimes suffering feels like you're talking to a crowd of a million people. Without a microphone. And you're now using only your loud outside voice.

You're standing up there on the stage. They see your mouth moving. But no amplified sound comes out. That stinks. Especially when you're suffering.

So you simply quit talking anymore. What's the use? But wait ... please don't quit.

Be clear about your real, legitimate needs. And distinguish those from your 'wants'.

There's a difference between them. "I want to get out of here" is real and felt and good to say. But "I need this or that because" ... that's more powerful.

And specific. And realistic. And negotiable. And workable. Together.

No one wants to be sick. No one wants to lie in some hospital or nursing home bed.

But some human 'needs' can be met along the way. Even there.

Suffering in silence isn't a good way along the way. When you do so, it's 'no way'.

Separate your specific needs from your wants. Hope and pray for the latter.

Be clear about the former. Then constructively articulate those needs to others.

Even when it's hard to do so. Even when you suffer pain and loss. It's your right.

Movement Eight:
Then Forgive Others When They're Not Met

"I told you. I told you a million times that I needed this from you.

It wasn't a ginormous 'ask'. It wasn't anything big. Just a small thing, really.

And then I waited. And waited. And waited. Then nothing. Oh yes, there was something. It was silence. Nothing, really."

Sometimes others betray our hopes and our confidence. We thought they heard us, were on board with us, were fighting for us, were on our side.

He was going to 'just do it' for me. He even said, "You can count on me."

"I did, but he didn't deliver. There was only silence. Nothing, really. Now I'm angry.

I'm angry at him and myself for trusting that guy. I'm angry with everyone, actually.

That's it. I'm on my own now. Can't trust anyone. Yep, betrayed."

But what if that anger is nothing more than another form of suffering? An added brick on the pile. A cancer that only adds to your misery. The slow and creepy kind.

Metastasizing. Slowly and steadily. Until it kills you.

Not you, but your heart. Your soul. Your spirit.

What if you chose *not* to tell that guy off? But tell him about how you feel about it?

Why it mattered to you. Why it still does. And why that guy still matters to you.

And what if you chose to stay connected to that guy? And you practiced grace.

Accepted that we are all only human. Full of other noise in our lives that gets in the way.

But we all wake each morning trying to do our best. Not to 'stick it' to others.

What if you assumed positive intent when that guy doesn't measure up fully?

He means well. Has a good heart. Let's keep talking and working together.

I need that guy. He needs me. Let's move on . . . with each other.

Movement Nine:
Scratched and Clawed

"Now she's really gone and done it."

"Do you believe it? That she really said that about me to my other friend?"

"That my brother did that? Behind my back? Do you believe it?"

"I am simply furious now. Beside myself. He went and did it. She went too far."

"He just slays me. She literally killed me with this."

"I'm gonna fight fire with fire. Tooth and nail. Going for the jugular. He'll get his."

"When I finally start to feel better. Get well. She'll get hers."

So, exactly what did your friend do? Your brother? Let me have a look.

"Oh, I see. A surface wound. It sounded a lot worse from your description.

I think you'll actually pull through. We'll patch that right up. Not life threatening."

When you're suffering, everything is magnified. When you hurt, you're vulnerable.

Grass fire. No, forest fire. No thanks to her.

I got scratched here. No, I got clawed. No thanks to him.

Glass half full. No, glass half empty. Actually, totally empty. No thanks to them.

Maybe it's that bad. Maybe it's not. If it's not, maybe it's you. No thanks to you.

What if you put it in perspective? Sat back and looked at it with some distance.

Maybe it only seemed or felt that bad? In the moment. At that time.

What if tomorrow it doesn't look that bad? With the benefit of a night's sleep.

Or by talking it through with another. Or by discerning the actual extent of the injury.

Or by giving others the benefit of the doubt. Even when you think they don't deserve it.

What if you patched up the surface wound?

And focused on something more healing.

Movement Ten:
Feeling Sorry For and Feeling With

"I must get over to see Peter at the hospital. He's been there for 3 weeks.

I don't really have the time, but it's the right thing to do. He got a bad break with his heart failure. I feel sorry for him. I pity his wife and kids. What a shame."

"Gotta stop by to briefly visit in case he . . . you know . . . doesn't make it. I won't be long. I'll take care of this and we'll go play tennis. Or golf. Or softball. Or go bowling."

"I feel so sorry for them. What a pity. Be back in a flash. Then we'll go."

Feeling sorry and pity for is not the same as 'feeling with.'

I can feel *with* someone only by also feeling their own pity and sorrow. By entering into it for a while. Sharing it in the moment. With them. Really with them.

Feeling sorry for is done at a distance. Arms length. A few paces away. Staying back.

Like when you feel sorry for old Joe, but don't want to catch whatever he has.

Or the neighbor who lost her legs in the war. "The whole thing makes me uncomfortable. I'll just call. Maybe send a card. What a pity. What a shame."

When you suffer, it's good to know the difference. Between being pitied and cared for.

When people feel sorry for you, you're an object. Other. They don't want to get too close to you. They don't want to feel uncomfortable. To sit with your pain. With you.

Feeling sorry for someone isn't necessarily bad. But it doesn't help all that much either.

It's like the express wash for your car. No waxing. No buffing. No wheel coat.

Your car knows the difference. You do, too, when you suffer.

Build friendships that do the deluxe car wash. Waxing. Buffing. Wheel coating.

Fully detailed. The whole works. Spend your suffering time *with* them.

Seek them out. Nurture them. Even as they nurture you. With you.

Movement Eleven:
Staying Connected—Touch and Sound

"We're hanging out together. Oh, yes we are. Taking in a movie. Going to the game."

"Going to lunch, to the bar, the concert, the picnic, the beach. Hanging out."

"Well not completely together, of course. You know how it goes. I need to check my email, my texts, my photos, my messages."

"I have demands on my life, you know." A lot going on. Too much, probably.

My smart phone, my smart TV, my smart computer. Lots of it.

My music, my music videos, my tunes, my play list. Lots of it.

I touch my screen, the touch screen. I scroll. I hit 'enter'. I hit 'delete'. Love that one.

Every so often, I look up and around. Are you still there? Let's keep hanging together.

This is fun. We're really connected. In the Cloud. Online. On the web. On the Net.

Yes, connected. *Not*. Not really at all. Nada connection. Circuit short-circuited.

High tech. High noise. High distraction. Low sound. Very low touch.

When we're suffering, we miss high touch a lot. Like the touch of a hug. A warm handshake. A gentle pat on the back. Someone holding our hand.

And we miss sounds. Human sound. A gentle voice. A soothing melody.

Especially when it comes from someone who holds my hand *while* she's talking with me. And especially when she's talking to me, not about me.

Especially when they're not talking about me quietly from elsewhere in the room. Like when I hear others discussing me . . . without me. "Even when you think I can't hear you. You apparently didn't get the memo. I can."

Loving touch and sounds matter. They matter a lot. Especially when you suffer.

Especially when that's about all that you have left. Glad we touched on this.

Movement Twelve: Unfinished Business

What am I most frightened about? About death. I don't want to die. I'm scared to death.

It's quite final, this dying. The final frontier. The final breath. The final goodbye.

"I don't know what to say to mother. If I tell her how I feel, it means that I've given up.

I need to help her keep fighting. Keep trying. Keep breathing. Keep living.

Not giving in, surrendering, or letting go. We need to keep fighting. No final words.

If I do, I'll cry. I'll be weak. I simply can't let mom see me suffering.

I have to be strong for her. Steady. Like a rock. No tears. Not now."

But what if gaining some closure was the best thing to do? While you can.

Telling another that you love them, will miss them enormously, but it's OK to let go.

What if you said the things that desperately need to be said. While you still can.

Like "I'm sorry for that." "I wish I could have done it differently. Forgive me."

Like "You were the best mother I could ever have wished for. Thank you."

Like "You made a real difference during your life. It's a better place because of you."

Like "Life won't be the same without you. But I will always love you."

Like getting unfinished business finally finished. Said. Finalized. Out in the open in love and grace. Because when we finish unfinished business, we say 'See Ya' to the Pink Elephant in the room. You know the one.

The one we know is always there . . . but the animal that we always try to ignore.

Even though it's there. In the room. Alongside the Emperor with no clothes. Really.

Finishing unfinished business helps us all to get rid of the elephant and get some closure. I mean healthy closure if it's done in love. It helps us to go on, let be, or let go.

To finalize things with love and with nothing else left out. Godspeed.

Post-Movement Reflection Questions

How are my notions and definitions of my own 'independence' creating or worsening my suffering? Why?

What 'stories' about myself and my life's meaning do I need to share with others right now? Why is that story important to my identity and my place in community with others?

How healthy are my boundaries with others at this time? Which boundary areas need to be re-examined to create healthier relationships in my time of pain and loss?

In what ways do I tend to 'stand back' when I see others who suffer? Why? How can I connect in more loving, present ways for them?

What unfinished business am I reluctant to 'finish' in order to gain greater closure or forgiveness? How is that reluctance actually weighing me down in ways that prevent my healing?

Post Movement Rest and Prayer

Loving God, thank you for bringing human help to my side in this time. Thank you for others who support me, love me, hold me, listen to me, and share with me. And sometimes carry me. I know they are your arms and legs and hands here, right here in the midst of my pain. In this time of suffering, I'm most acutely aware of the importance of our connectedness as a human community. In shared stories. And in shared communion. Even in the throes of my pain, might you help me to see things more clearly. Might you give me the words to better articulate my needs to others. Help me to see that my wants may not always be possible now, but that my needs can be met. Help me to know the difference between feeling hurt and being truly hurt by others. And help me to more readily forgive others for unmet needs and the hurts that I experience. Please bring others of goodwill and loving hearts to my side. Help them to truly hear me, sit with me, and connect with me in deeply spiritual ways on this journey. Help us to stay connected in love, even when I can't speak, move, smile, or even stay awake. And help me and those around me to say the things that matter most. To finish the unfinished. To gain closure that heals no matter what. To express feelings with hearts of grace, peace, and love. Their's and mine. In all these things, might we enter, live, and leave this world together as a family. A family borne of common bloodline. Common hopes and fears. Common interests. Common needs. Acted out through uncommon, lasting, communal bonds. Together. Thank you, God.

Chapter Six

Where are my Hope and my Deliverance?

"There is light in this world, a healing spirit more powerful than any darkness we may encounter. We sometimes lose sight of this force when there is suffering, too much pain. Then suddenly, the spirit will emerge through the lives of ordinary people who hear a call and answer in extraordinary ways."

—MOTHER TERESA

Pre-Movement Stretch

When we suffer, we want not just relief. Not just the pain to go away. For a while. We want to see real, lasting pockets of hope. We want to know what's the point of it all. What difference it makes in me. And what's next. Not tomorrow or next week or next month. But much farther down the road. Even when I'm not on it any longer. If so, where will I be? With whom? Doing what? In the out-of-my-body future state. In my new, 'permanent' address. That matters a lot. And it should. For, in the span of eternity, we walk this earth for a short time only. Where we came from matters. So does where we're going. Both now and after we've 'gone'. In the pages ahead, we'll explore the here-now and hereafter. Using my own Christian tradition as a framework, we'll look at the Reign of God. We'll explore the difference between this and Heaven. Then, we'll challenge our notions of Heaven, as we know it now. In so doing, we'll look at ways in which 'heaven' happens right now. While we're actually here. And how God might use *this* place, not our preconceived notions of Heaven, as our landing spot in the future. As we move, we'll re-think our notions of God as our final destination Judge and Juror. Challenge what it means to be 'saved'. And offer a potentially affirming, healthier vision of our own 'resurrection' in the future. One that's more inclusive in potentially provocative, but interesting, ways. One that takes the best of us and of all things in ways that build a truly loving, just Reign of God. Where God's plan and purpose for us all are fully fulfilled. In all their lasting glory. In all their lasting love. In all their lasting hope.

Movement One:
Sunrise/Sunset

The old man walked nearly the entire day. It was unusually hot and humid. Perspiration beaded on his forehead, and he wiped his brow with his wrinkled, damp shirt. He was short of breath and feeling a bit faint. The sun was creeping slowly from east to west in the northern skies. As it crawled toward the horizon, though, the intensity of the heat lessened. The sharper angle of the sunlight provided more shade by trees and branches along the path. Patches of breeze began to cool his worn body. Nonetheless, he felt his fatigue deeply, and walked toward the shoreline. The old man found a large flat rock on the sand, and was grateful for a chance to finally rest for the day.

He sat quietly and dozed off for some time. As his eyes opened again, he thought it strange that he had not fallen over as he slept. He longed to lie down for the night, but was drawn to the horizon. So he continued to simply sit. The old man smiled as the sun eased to the bottom of the western sky. The brilliant blue of the day's skies became darker and more pronounced. The sun's rays skipped along the water before him, like twinkling, dancing lights. He stared at them for some time, almost in a trance. So much so, that he didn't hear the sound of someone approaching. A stranger walked toward the man and asked to sit with him for a while. Although exhausted from the day, the old man extended his arm to a spot in the sand near him. The stranger eased to the sand and said, "It looks like you found the only comfortable seat here. You're sitting on my favorite rock."

The old man felt uneasy with this, not clear on how to respond. He replied, "I won't be long here, as I need to sleep soon. I'll keep your rock warm in the meantime." They each laughed for a moment, then silence ensued. Both looked outward and upward to the western sky. The sun now approached the horizon. It appeared to have grown quite large as it dipped to a spot now just above the water line. Brilliant orange and red colors leapt from this enormous circle of light in the sky. Its shape began to contort some on the edges, making it appear to be emanating powerful energies outward toward the waters just below it as it sank. It was a magnificent show in the sky, dazzling to the eye and the heart.

The stranger turned to the old man and asked, "Which do you like more, the sunrise or sunset?" The old man answered quickly, "The sunrise." The stranger reflected for just a second and came back, "Interesting. Why so?" The man replied, "Yes, it is interesting. Actually, I love the sunset. It's something to behold, perhaps the prettiest thing in the world to watch. I love it, but it also makes me sad." The stranger was now perplexed. She said, "Sad is a powerful emotion. How can one be sad in the face of such magnificent beauty?" The old man offered, "I'm happy, then I'm sad. You see, the sunset makes me happy. But it marks an end. The end of the day. It brings dusk and then darkness immediately in its wake. And the dark of night is my most difficult time. Endings and darkness make me sad."

The stranger nodded as she listened intently to the old man. After a brief pause, she asked, "Yes, sunsets bring an end to the day. But are they really the end?" The old man replied, "They are for me." "What comes after the sunset," asked the stranger? The man came back, "I guess darkness and sometimes the moon rises on the other horizon." "Yes," the stranger affirmed. "And the different, but also brilliant, light that it brings to the night skies. And furthermore, the sun is rising somewhere else in the world as it sets for us." The old man placed his arm and hand under his chin, now resting it on a new foundation. He replied, "I guess you're right in that. But I can't see the sun rising somewhere else. All I see is it setting." The stranger looked to the sky and said, "The fact that we don't see it doesn't mean that it's not there. It is. The sunset means that we're simply sharing the sun with someone else someplace else for a while. It's not really an ending. In fact, there isn't an ending or a beginning. The sun is always rising and setting for someone in the world every minute. It's in constant motion. It's a matter of continuity and continuous life, not some abrupt ending to our own lives. Things continue to continue."

The old man smiled and turned toward the stranger. "That makes sense. Here's an interesting thought. What if the sunset that we saw tonight carries the wonder and joyfulness of our own hearts to those watching it set somewhere else right now? You know, pulls in our awe and loving wonder as we watched it set—and gives it to someone else enjoying this moment right after us?" The stranger thought on that for a minute. She replied, "Perhaps you're right. We share not only the sunset but also the love of that sunset. Passing it along to one another. And here's another thought. What if the sunset also shares the hope of *tomorrow's* sunrise? As if the sunset bears in itself the seeds of hope for a new day?"

The old man began to rise from the rock. He turned to the stranger and thanked her for their shared time together. He said, "You know, I think I like sunsets the best now. They bring the promise of tomorrow, built on the wonder of the night before." The stranger shook the old man's hand and smiled. They parted, each taking one more look at the now dark horizon.

Movement Two:
The Reign of God—Right Now

In my faith tradition, the 2nd Testament Gospels teach us that Jesus talked about the Kingdom of God. In fact, he did it a lot. Real important stuff to him. And to us.

Actually, I prefer the Reign of God. Kingdom conjures up all kinds of things.

Kingdom equals power and possession. Kings are male. Kings sit on thrones.

You know, the big ones in big palaces in big, gorgeous rooms.

The thrones sit up higher than the rest of us. So we can feel subservient and small.

We know how it goes. The King issues decrees from on high.

The little minions obey from below. Kingdom rule: Kings decree. Subjects obey.

But 'Reign' is different. It means that we're part of a new order. Something different. Strikingly so. Out there. Off our grid. Another way. Everyone come on in.

Jesus Christ announced the Reign of God. He also *did* it with love and healing and grace. A way of peace. Something radical. Real actions. Not just words.

He turned our notion of 'kingdom' on its head. Then asked us to come into his head.

And heart. Out there. In there. With him. With each other. Together.

"Now that's all well and good. The whole Reign thing sounds like a winner.

Someday, I suppose. But I've got real problems right now. Remember, I'm suffering.

I won't be around for the Reign, anyway. I'm on my last legs right now."

But what if the Reign is right now too, though? Right here. Step right up.

And the Reign of God is hanging around us in our real lives? Not just the ones that we'll have after we . . . . Clear throat . . . . "Die. Like after I pass on."

What if God's Reign is already working in the midst of our suffering? Building you up and those around you. Consider yourself invited. Everyone welcome. Informal attire.

Movement Three:
Been Here, Done That

"So, I kind of get this Reign thing. It sounds good in theory. Right now in our midst.

But give me something to hang this all on. Something real and practical. Past evidence."

In my faith tradition, we honor a God of both the 1st and 2nd Testaments of the Bible.

Though, we can get pretty hung up with the 2nd Testament Cross and Resurrection thing around Christ. It's easy to forget that Jesus was actually *doing* his Reign thing while he was here in the flesh with us. Not just lip service. Not some rainy day fund for down the road. Not some travel insurance policy for stormy weather in the future.

He was actually doing the hard Reign work. Wearing down the leather on his dusty sandals. Then cleaning his feet as he readied for the next dusty walk.

Going the extra mile to carry it out. Just doing it. Every day. Every minute.

Further, God was *already* at work in the Bible's 1st Testament, *before* Christ. Doing crazy stuff like rescuing God's people out of slavery in Egypt. And ensuring they had food and sustenance while they journeyed to God's promised place. And teaching them about justice and fairness and love and community and generosity and grace.

And coming along for the ride. Yes, coming along. Like a Reign tour guide.

This whole Reign thing has been in overdrive for some time, then.

Since the whole creation scene. When God put the world and life and us together.

Since the beginning. That means since forever ago. This means that the hope and plan of God's Reign is not some Plan B for screwed-up humans. It WAS and IS the plan. The Plan A. For us. Forever. It's especially the Plan A when we suffer. It's the Plan A that tells us that God is working in our pain and loss. Along for the ride. Past and present.

Someone and something to hold onto. Something building, not dying.

Movement Four:
Future Promise

"This Reign thing isn't beaming through very strongly at the moment. It's not making my pain and grief go away. Comforting, yes. Fully transforming, I can't say yet.

Not seeing it yet. Not fully yet. Yet. I'm holding on the line. Tapping my fingers on the table. Still waiting. So, tell me again about this future promise of God's Reign . . . "

We're a right now, have it my way, make it real to me, in the moment kind of world.

"God, the future Reign downloading thing is taking way too long. I need faster broadband. I don't have all day. Please speed up the future promise. I'm suffering."

But God has a different wavelength. God doesn't see time and space in the same way that we do. The Reign has been here, in part. It's here right now, in part. It's been slowly building. But we've not yet closed on the house. It's under construction. On-track because a loving God is the prime contractor. But it's not yet finished. Nor are we. That's why we call it a *future* promise. That's why we need faith and hope. Sometimes, it feels like God's left the building site. Sometimes, it looks like things are heading in the wrong direction completely. With myself, my family, my community, and the world. But God is working. Building. No extended vacations or holidays. So, keep your eye on the building plans, not just the construction site itself. And admit that you don't have God's 3-D safety glasses and smart watch. That's why we call it a future hope. That's why we need faith and courage and perseverance to stay with it.

We may not attend the new house-warming party in our own lifetimes. But we'll be invited in some form or fashion. When the future promise is fully realized.

God will stand before us and bless this house—and say, "I told you it would happen. Welcome home. Step inside. Quite a place we've built together, don't you think?"

Movement Five:
We're All in it Together

So, it's quite a Reign we're building together.

The operative word is *together*. Something's truly wrong when I push my co-workers off the building site. Or put a claim on my bedroom before the place is finished. Or order furniture to my taste only. Or draw up the guest list for the Reign-warming party when it's time to close on the house. You know, the short-list of special guests. My list. The guests who get the trendy Champagne. The bubbly in cut-glass sippy cups.

"We'll have a tent outside for the others. With port-a-potties. Serving lemonade.

Only enough space inside the place for the in-crowd. The few, the proud, the special people. The One Percent. Don't want to over-crowd the living room."

Something tells me this isn't what God has in mind for God's Reign. God makes it 'Reign' on all people. God has a much larger guest list. Wants to invite all those who built the place, not just those who financed the construction. Think of it as a mega block party. With plenty of good food and drink for everyone. Eating together.

And God has built the place to be handicapped accessible. Nice ramps. Good layout. We all have our disabilities. All of us. Even when we can't afford the best doctors. God wants us to come, even if we're limping, walking with a cane, pushing a walker. Or getting wheeled in. Especially then. Wants us to simply get there with faith and love and hope on the way. No matter how long it takes to do that.

We're not talking Last Call. Or First Call. No, indeed. It's an 'All Call'.

Suit and tie not required. Just bring your heart and love for God and the other guests.

Every hour is happy hour. When the Reign comes fully in the future. For us.

Mark your collective calendars. Don't yet have a date. So keep your 'tomorrows' open.

Movement Six:
What About our World?

So, this Reign thing, our hope, is building as we go. It's gonna be a big block party of love one day. Big tent. Lots of folks from lots of places. Good. No, Great.

"Can't wait for this wing-ding to get fully going. Even though I'm in pain, it gives me some hope. My life and love and contributions have helped build the new place.

That should matter for something. I'm starting to feel it . . . "

"Now, how do I get *there*? There. It can't be here. No way, here. This place is a mess.

Beam me up in the end. Up. Yes, up. That's where heaven is, isn't it? Up there."

"This old world is beyond repair. Let's abandon it. Let someone else have it.

We're all outta here in the new Reign. This Reign needs a fresh start somewhere else.

I need a fresh start somewhere else. I want to leave my pain and suffering behind me."

But what if God's promised place isn't somewhere else? Not something else?

What about this world? The one that God made . . . way back when.

Why would God give up on God's very creation; the one God put all that effort into in the first place? Then gave it to us to manage. Remember?

As if God's sure to get us all away from here, then put the old, beleaguered homestead up for sale. Like, "Price Reduced. It's a fixer-upper. Would somebody take this off my hands? Please. I'll even throw in the furniture and the animals. And the landscaping."

What if God's Reign was to happen right here? No sale. We're staying.

What if God is somehow building something better, right here in our midst?

With the loving and positive, difference-making things, moments, and actions that sometimes happen here? Right here.

Even if we can't see God working behind the scenes.

Movement Seven:
Heaven as a Destination

"Get onboard. The Heaven train is leaving. Don't delay. You'll be left behind."

That means you. The one waiting in line for the hotdog and soda. Or at the gift store buying a souvenir for the trip. Or on your phone saying "Goodbye. See ya. Will send a postcard from the heavenly gates. Wish you were here, kind of."

"Oh, and this Reign place is going to be truly amazing. I hear they have music, bingo, dancing, golf, swimming, and tennis. Probably a spa, too. Called the 'Heavenly Touch'.

And the best beach going. With the best chase lounges. And the best umbrella drinks.

What a place! I don't care how I get there. I just want to get there. And live the life . . .

I'll hang out with all my old, long-departed relatives and friends. Something to behold.

I'm all in. I'm down with this whole thing. Ah, I mean 'up'. Just get me through the gates. The Pearly Gates. Then I'm in. In. Forever. Resort living without the bills.

Finally, some relief from my suffering. Finally."

In God's fully realized Reign, there'll be no more suffering, pain, and death. That was never God's plan in the first place. But God might be building it *here*. Yeah, here.

That means that it's not a 'destination'—a place to get out from underneath 'living'. Not a far-away resort for us. You know, the 'Heaven-Sent Lodge'. Nope.

In that case, the Reign isn't a ticket out, but a place *in*. To be part of something amazing here someday . . . however that 'part of' is constituted. In. Really in.

What if the most important thing is that we're all finally part of God's plan and purpose?

In God's fully present love and light. To be with and in God fully. Where we'll all be joined in some amazing ways that we can't even imagine on this side of the Reign. Shouldn't that be more than enough for us? Especially when we've suffered.

Movement Eight: Heaven as our Being

"So, now you've done it. You've ruined the trip I've planned to heaven. Without my ticket outta here, I've got nothing after my 'end' here. Nada. Zilch. Last breath, curtain goes down. Sweep up the aisles. Nothing left here. Oh, and turn out the lights."

Now, this whole leaving here for Heaven isn't a bad thing in itself. Perhaps, that's what will happen. Maybe we'll someday get zoomed up, get a new supercharged body, and live forever. Leave all the crummy stuff behind us in our wake. Not a bad thing.

But I don't think that's what God has in mind for us. What use were we here then?

So, what if we all lived a little bit of heaven right *here*? While we're actually living here.

Heaven like the awe and wonder of a sunset. Or the warmth of summer's breeze. The laughter of children. The beauty of a blooming flower. The brilliant colors of autumn leaves. The touch of someone who loves you. The grace and forgiveness of your friend, when you messed up big-time. Yep, the time you'd rather forget. The sound of a soft, caring voice. The hug of a parent or relative. The joy of doing something really fun and crazy for the first time. Your first kiss. Your first ice cream cone.

When we get so fixed on that 'other' place, we lose the heaven that's already in our lives.

The place where we live now. That lives in us. That *is* us. Yes, us. From God.

Because why would God make us just to punish us, and test us, and give us a lot of grief? Just so we'd look forward to the 'other' place someday?

Who does that? Especially when God loves you. Especially when you're suffering.

When you make a place for God and others in *this* world, you enter into a little bit of heaven right here. Maybe not all of it, but some part of it.

So, look around. Look inside. Enjoy a slice . . . of heaven. To-day. Now.

Movement Nine:
Hell—Here Comes the Judge

Can we go back to that Pearly Gates part? The part about someone standing at the gate of Heaven. With the checklist of good things and bad things I've done. Score sheet. Probably an algorithm of some sort that calculates a total ranking for us. And we hear,

"I'm very sorry . . . but you've not met the minimum cut-point. Thanks for playing the Game of Life. Here's your lovely parting gift. My angel will see you to the door . . . to that 'other' place. Please take everything with you. You'll be staying in Hell. Forever.

Dress in layers down there. You'll want to peel off your clothes when they turn up the furnace. Which, by the way, they do all the time. It's really hot. Do you burn easily? I know you've suffered a lot already, but I can't let everyone in here. Just a few. Oh, did I mention that you'll meet the Devil in Hell? Watch your back. Have a nice forever."

And to think we'd had to live with this hanging over our heads our whole lives. Who does this kind of thing to God's people? Why have we made God into some kind of mean, old Judge? Who sits on a throne and passes sentence on us. And who says, "So, you get eternal life. And you, yes you, get death by fire. It's one way *or* another. Life *or* death. No appeal process, by the way. Take him away. That door, not this one, for her."

But what if there's another way? Like God is not a Judge at the end. But discerns with us those ways we've done good or bad or some things in-between. Helps us to understand, with the fullness of God's wisdom and heart and grace. Both now . . . *and* in the end. And uses the good stuff to build the Reign. And brings the light God placed in us into God's loving embrace. Both now and after we've passed from this place. What if it's not an either-or? Not an all or nothing?

What about some part of, to be blended with something else? Mixed gently with love.

Movement Ten:
Saved by the Bell

In my Christian faith tradition, we often talk about being saved. By God. To God.

Saved by our accepting Jesus Christ as our Lord and Savior. Saved.

I honor those who feel they've been saved. I listen with respect and joy as they tell their stories of the day, moment, and point in their lives. I, however, can't point to such a day. To a specific event. To a moment when I turned to God, confessed my sinfulness, and asked for Christ to come into my life. Not one thing. Not one day. Not one defining, deafening crescendo. No cymbals. No drum roll. No blast from the trumpets. No heavenly choir. Sorry . . . I didn't make it to the big show. But I'm saved anyway.

Saved each and every moment. One at a time. By God. I didn't come to that in an hour, in a day, in a week, on a retreat, at the altar, outside the church, in the night.

No, not that way. It came slowly into my heart. Over years. Despite my disinterest at the time. I was busy. My *phone* was busy. "Sorry, God. Tied up. Call ya later."

But God had me on speed dial. Kept gently speaking to me . . . without words. Just being there. No amazing dreams, no gigantic ahh-haas, no flashy pronouncements from the heavens. No hearing strange voices. No sirens. No near misses. No fireworks.

Just God. Wordless, gentle rustling of my heart. God let me know that someone was there, who wanted me, would stay with me, love me for who I was. God stayed with me, sat with me, lied awake with me. Cried with me. Prayed with me. Held onto me when I couldn't sleep. Loved me. Brought friends to me. Brought help and comfort.

And saved me. From my pain, my sorrow, and even myself.

Slowly and imperceptibly. When I started picking up the phone. God calling.

A loving voice was on the other end. "Glad we can finally talk. I love you."

Movement Eleven:
Saved by Myself

"If only I were a better person. If only I prayed harder. If only I hadn't screwed up.

If only, if only, if only, if only. I. I. I. I. I coulda, shoulda, woulda done more."

It's easy to blame ourselves when things are going poorly. When we're feeling poorly.

And we get lots of help on that score. "The line forms over there for all those wanting to pile on. Yes, way back there. It's now wrapped around the building three times. Everyone keep the line moving, please. Please have your blame cards and snappy lines out of your wallets, ready for the suffering guy in the bed. He needs to make more effort here. Needs a bit of a push, if you know what I mean. Actually, he needs a good kick."

Or at least it can seem that way to us. If only, if only, if only, if only. I. I. I. I.

Now, we're all accountable for what we've done and not done. We bear some part.

But heaping blame is not the answer. Especially when we heap it on ourselves. Or let others do so. Heap blame for our suffering. For our predicament. For our losses.

And trying harder, praying harder, working harder, thinking harder isn't the answer either . . . Not if we think that's the only, best answer. All the time . . .

And not when it becomes a cause of further suffering and guilt when things don't work out as we'd like. And we hear things like, "I'm sorry to report that Suzie lost her battle with heart failure last night." Stop it. It's not helpful. At all. Quit blaming Suzie.

Suzie didn't 'lose' her battle with this terrible disease. She returned to God following her struggle with it. She tried and tried and tried. It wasn't her fault. She didn't *lose*.

She didn't fail. She got sick and died. She tried hard. But the illness took its course.

So let's quit saying she 'lost'. Let's quit implicitly blaming her for her weakness.

Let's just comfort others in that loss. And let's pray for Suzie.

Movement Twelve: Resurrection

"And they all lived happily ever after . . .

What a happy, happy ending. So, in the end, they all got raised up into Heaven. All of them. Just like that. Well, most of them. Actually, some of them. Few of them?

Feel badly for the ones God left behind. Gonna be trouble for them. For sure."

Jesus Christ rose after his crucifixion. I believe that fervently as a Christian. He was of God to start with. And returned to his place in the Holy Trinity. He returned to his eternal beginning. Perhaps we'll be raised in the end, too. Nothing wrong with that.

Unless we make it our mission. Correction, *my* mission . . . my *individual* mission.

"Yep, just get me in the lifeboat and let's motor outta here. And head to where 'I'll' be safe forever." Operative word: 'I'. *All* of me. 'Me, Me, Me, Me, Me'.

Like a gang of kids with their hands in the air screaming for candy. *Their* candy. But what if there's another way? A way where our love, our faith, our grace, our actions, and our light get resurrected. Remember, for the building project. The Reign.

Where God welcomes those things back. While we're here and after we're gone.

And uses those things that God gave us in the first place to make things better in the end.

Things like when we forgave our neighbor, brought food to a sick friend, donated to the poor, prayed for another, loved our family, fought for our dog's life, took in a rescue cat. And things like the brilliant light of our faith . . . in spite of our suffering. The light that would simply not go out. The one that was fueled by God in the first place.

For it was never really ours to start with. It was God's gift to us. While we were here.

Then all of it went back to God.

Where it's sorted and used where God wants it. Resurrected.

Post-Movement Reflection Questions

What if I stopped waiting for heaven 'some day' and tried to live far more of it today?

How can I become more inclusive in my view of my fellow humanity? How can I begin to see salvation as a more omni-expandable proposition where all are wanted within our family of God?

What things can I do to better see *all* creation (plants, animals, our environment) as sacred and loved by God—not just human beings?

In what unhealthy ways am I judging myself and others, while attributing this judgment to God? How can I change that judgment to more unconditional love?

How can I better let go of my need to control myself and others in God's name—then simply let God 'be'?

Post-Movement Rest and Prayer

Loving God, thank you for the promise of a better tomorrow. Thank you for my hope for deliverance. From my suffering, my loss, my sorrows, and my pain. But, thank you also for life in all that it brings . . . today. It's good to know that my life counts for something now, not just sometime future. That it counts right here, not just somewhere else far away. Even my pain and suffering has meaning. And it's comforting to know that you're working in the midst of that suffering and in those who work to relieve it. That you've been working to liberate, comfort, deliver, and give life since the very start of time. Your Reign is therefore past, present, and future. I pray, God, that I might hope not simply for myself. But for others. Others who suffer. Others who help those who suffer. And for our world. Our world suffers, too. And it longs for deliverance from the many things that try to destroy it. God, I pray, even in my pain, that I might know you and your love more fully. While I know that I'm accountable for my actions, my mistakes, and the impacts of those things, I pray that your grace and presence will reign. Reign above all else. You have saved me by simply creating me. And staying with me. And continuing to call me to yourself. That's why I was made. To be with others and with you. Together. Saved. Together. Might all things be resurrected to you, both living and dead. To be used to your good ends and plan. And in that, might I always be with you. As I was before. As I am now. As I will be in the future. With and in You. Thank you, God.

Chapter Seven

Re-Defining Forward Movement

"Contrary to what we may have been taught to think, unnecessary and unchosen suffering wounds us but need not scar us for life. What we allow the mark of suffering to become is in our own hands."

—BELL HOOKS

Pre-Movement Stretch

Suffering isn't an academic, theoretical, or esoteric exercise. To be fair, thinking more broadly about our suffering *is* important. Doing so puts a framework around it. It gives our pain some meaning. It helps us to cope, to manage, to heal, and to hope. It helps us to understand our sorrows and our losses more deeply. That all matters. But sometimes what we need most is help in *this* moment. Another way forward today. Right now. Practical, really usable things that help us take our next step, take our next breath, take our next pill, take a break, or take a bit more control. Right now. In the pages ahead, we'll move onto those more concrete things. We'll acknowledge that suffering brings real losses. Things we now live without. But we'll also explore things we can live 'with'. Even in our pain. Helpful, healing things we can keep *with* us through the pain and sorrow. Things we can work with, not toss out. Things we can learn from. Like questions, impermanence, inclusivity, options, descriptions not labels, silence, prayerfulness, and mindfulness. We'll look at living 'with' your real, truest self through it all. And with goodbyes when it's time. With the promise that no ' Everlasting Hell' waits for you. But where God always waits for you. Right by your side. Where you'll therefore 'live' with hope in your midst. Hope you can hang your future on. Undying hope. Everlasting hope. Real hope.

Movement One:
Friendly Trade Winds

The old man walked, seemingly for hours, along the path. It was mid-day, and he left the trail for the beach. As he reclined to the sand, he noticed the breeze against his cheek. More so than usual today. He was grateful for it. The winds brought relief from the heat of the afternoon sun. It made for more restful sleep at night. The sound of the wind was steady and comforting. It was always there. Sometimes it blew against his face. Sometimes it brushed his side. Sometimes it pushed him forward on the path. But it was always there. Always coming from the same direction. It didn't change. He did. As he turned right, it brushed him to the side. As he turned left, it brushed his forehead. As he turned away, it brushed him along. Always there. It didn't change direction. He did.

As he rested and pondered, a stranger approached from behind. The stranger sat beside him, taking a few breaths. "Been a day," the person offered. "Quite a breeze. Could start blowing harder tonight from the looks of the sky." The old man was especially tired today. He found it difficult to summon a lot of words. But he noticed that the wind made it easier to breath. It was as if the breeze came into his lungs without his own efforts. Breathing almost for him. Forcing its way in, but not in a bad way. Actually breathing with him. That made it less work for him. The man turned toward the stranger and said, "Yes, quite a breeze. It never stops blowing. Sometimes softer. Sometimes harder. But always blowing. Carries one along with it, I guess."

The stranger smiled and replied, "Yes. In its wake. Best not to fight it. Best to work with it. In it. Become a part of it, if you know what I mean." The old man lowered his head for a moment and said, "I guess. But it always blows from the same direction. Or, at least it seems that way. So, how do you work with it when you have to move against it sometimes?" The stranger moved a little closer to the old man and said, "When you get to know it better, you let it guide you. It helps you to navigate. Steady. Yes, she's steady, that wind. When I listen to the wind on my body, I know which direction I'm heading. Even when I'm moving against it, I know where I'm heading. The wind tells me. To my face. It's like a compass without a dial. I read it on my face, not with my eyes."

The old man pondered that for a while. He came back, "So, the prevailing winds push you along, pull you backwards, and move you sideways. And still, they always guide you? Help you to navigate?" The stranger offered, "Yes, as long as you work with them. Respect their right to blow as hard or softly as they want to. Let them do their thing and go with them, I guess. They're steady. I need to be more flexible in response to them." The old man reflected and replied, "And let them in." The stranger didn't understand. She said, "What do you mean 'in'?" The old man smiled and responded, "Let them in. Make them a part of you. Not like something outside of you. Let them enter into your body. Breath for you. Cool you off. Blow you along when you're tired. Those kinds of things. Make the winds your friend instead of only someone working for you."

"Interesting," the stranger offered. "But how do you invite the wind inside of you," she asked? "You trust it," the old man replied firmly, in turn. The stranger's interest was peaking. She questioned, "How do you trust the wind? The wind is a thing, an 'it', not a person." The old man scratched his head and turned to the stranger. He said, "Why not? It gives life and breath. It gives direction. It gives motion. It's always with us. Who's to say that it's not a gift from someone else? For us. Who's to say that it doesn't have life? In itself. Who's to say that we can't adopt it, befriend it, and be grateful for it? Make it part of ourselves. Who's to say that we have to control it, use it, or battle against it? What if we simply accept it? For what it is. Maybe not even an 'it'. But a friend. A real, dependable, steady friend. One that prevails. Blows the same direction every day. Sometimes hard. Sometimes softly. Sometimes almost imperceptibly. But always there. Always steady."

"Huh," the stranger replied. "Maybe you're right. I have to think on it a bit more," the stranger offered. She then said, "Good to talk with you. Good to be with you. But I must move on. The day is short. And I need to make more progress before the sun goes down. Are you moving on now, too?" The old man shook his head. He offered, "No, I'm going to sit for awhile. Take in the breeze for a bit longer. It feels good. Yes, I'm going to sit here and watch the sun go down." The stranger paid her respects and headed off. The old man sat, strangely relaxed and at peace. He would resume the path tomorrow. Time was not all that short in this moment.

Movement Two:
Living with Questions

When we suffer, we're seeking answers. Lots of them. "Bring them, please."

Specific, practical, actionable, informational, hopeful. Yeah, hang my hat on that one.

Like why is this happening . . . to me . . . right now? How do I make it better? How do we get on top of this thing? When is my life returning to normal, again? Back on track.

And how will my life change because of it? Will it ever go back to the way it was?

"You know, when things were like they used to be? Maybe they weren't so great, but I got comfortable with it, I guess. At least I was living with it. I had some answers."

But what if *the* answers aren't in the cards at the moment? Perhaps never again.

What if the good old days aren't coming back? Perhaps never again.

Can you live with that? The new 'normal'. A normal filled with more questions than answers? Questions to us . . . from us or even from God. To us.

Questions like how you'll reinvent yourself. And embrace change, even when it's scary.

Stay open to the unknown. Wrestle with it, live with it, even sit with it. Ponder on it. Reflect on it. Plan for it. Grow with it. Change with it.

Even heal with it. Enter into it. Be one with it. Yes, the unknown . . . the questions.

What if living the questions was more powerful than having the answers?

Finding some purpose and meaning in the ???s. Yes, the ???. Wherever they come from.

Thinking about us, our lives, our goals, and our happiness in new, expanded ways.

Seeking release and joyfulness in unanswered mysteries. Deep, abiding questions.

We are informed by answers. But may not be enlightened. And may not gain wisdom.

We're stretched and pushed and deepened by questions, even if we're not informed.

Especially when we suffer. When we think we need answers the most. Maybe we don't.

Movement Three:
Living with Imprecision

"So, Ms. Jones, I place your odds of a full and complete recovery at 60%."

"Based on the tests that we've run, the tumor has grown 35% over the last year."

"We can say with near certainty (90%) that this was caused by a genetic mutation."

"The accident investigation places the two cars colliding at exactly 65 mph. The car hitting your son's jumped the median divider at 9:30 pm. I'm so sorry for your loss."

We live in a cause and effect kind of world. Things happen for a reason. Precise ones.

If this, then that. If that, then this. The intersection of forces caused a chain reaction, resulting in this outcome. But for those things, these things wouldn't have happened. "80% sure of that, by my calculations. Almost precisely, I may add . . . "

And sometimes we *can* know those things. Clarity brings some closure. Some way to explain the inexplicable. Allows us to know 'why' and begin moving on with precision.

But sometimes we can't. Precisely because there are no reasons, answers, calculations, odds, estimates, or hypotheses. Not even an equation. Or a plausible theory or idea.

That's when it's harder to bear our suffering. Not knowing 'why' isn't just a question. It's a lingering wound that doesn't want to close. If only we knew why, we could start to understand. Start to move forward. With an exact reason for this pain.

But what if things just happen at times? Coincidence. Bad timing. A terrible break. Wrong place at the worst possible time. Wrong time at the worst possible place. Worst.

Unfair, unexplained, unjust, unreasonable, unsolved. Simply 'un'.

Imprecision happens. It just does sometimes. And it hurts. But when we begin to accept that, we can shed the need to control it all. Explain it all. Know it all. Measure it all.

Shed the burden that can't be lifted, except by us. When we slowly let go of it.

Movement Four:
Living with Impermanence

"That thing is built to last. Strong foundation. Solid beams. Rock solid."

"Engraved right there, over there, on the walk of fame. Will last a lifetime.

Perhaps forever. Long after I'm gone. Permanent. Lasting. Etched in stone."

We like to hang onto things and places and people. Hold them close. Make them last.

We acquire them, use them, hold them, maintain them, polish them, clean them.

Put them on the mantel. Display them. Brag about them. Tell stories about them.

Protect them from others. Fence them. Guard them. Mind them. Make 'em last.

We act as if things and relationships and accomplishments are trophies. Forever stuff.

"Can't wait to get this new car in my garage." This new friend. This trophy.

But what if we don't need a garage? A storage shed. A book-shelf. A trophy case.

What if nothing is forever? What if all things are perishable? Have a sell-by date?

Everything, except our own inner light and love. Our God-given grace. And those things we've done to make this place safer, kinder, more just, freer, and more loving.

The real treasures that fuel our true selves. The permanent stuff. No sell-by date here.

The selves that God made when God made us. The permanent stuff. Enjoy forever.

What if we focused on something new? Something lasting. An inside, outside job.

And what if this made our suffering a little easier? The pain won't last. Not forever. Even if it feels right now like it will. It won't. It's not permanent.

We don't have to live with it, make it a badge of honor or courage. We don't have to store it in our garage. It is a thing. It's not even me. It's not even them.

It's not permanent. Things come and things go. Suffering comes and goes.

But God wants to come and stay. And forgive. And love. Permanently.

Movement Five:
Living with Options

"Welcome to our show today. Our lucky contestant will now choose Door 1, Door 2, or Door 3." But here's the catch. We're changing it up. She'll know what's behind each door *before* she chooses. Best to know what it is. Lock it in. Go with it. Stay with it. Fix on it. Don't waver, second-guess, overthink, or let any doubt creep in. Door 1. That's that.

"And let's see what the lady's won." Door 1. That one. The one she picked. Forget about the others. Behind Door 1- her plans, her hopes, her ambitions, her goals, her strategy. Yes, it's all there behind *that* Door. All fixed.

She's picked it and she's sticking with the pick. Door 1.

But what happens when the Doors in our lives get mixed up? Like, we picked Door 1, only to find out that it isn't available any longer. "I had my mind and heart set on Door 1, only to have it pulled out from under me. Door 2 is a mystery. Door 3 isn't what I wanted most. I'm miserable about this. Cheated. Hoodwinked. Betrayed."

When we get sick, lose a loved one, live with pain, it feels like Door 1 was lifted.

Stolen. Taken from us. Now lost forever. Like the old bait-and-switch game. Gone.

And it feels easier to fix on the Door now gone missing. On what is 'no longer'. Gone.

"If I just stay with the pick, something might change. Magic might happen. Door 1 might return, be restocked, come off of lay-away. It could actually happen, you know."

But waiting for Door 1 may not be the best choice. Door 2 or Door 3 may not seem like the best prizes for us. Especially when we're grieving the loss of Door 1.

But staying open to Door 2 or 3 or even 4 or 5 might be the best we've got.

And doing our best with these Doors might turn out OK, after all . . .

Movement Six:
Living with Inclusivity

"That's the way it is. It's the way I was taught. The way I was brought up."

"It's the truth, the whole truth, and nothing but the truth. The whole one."

"That other stuff is hogwash. It's of the devil. Yes, the work of the devil."

"Close my ears. Close my eyes. Get me outta here. Don't want to be even tainted by it."

Sometimes, we like to think there is *a* way. Not a better way. Or an equally good way.

But *the* way. The only way. The one and only way. The rest is blasphemy . . . or worse.

Like if we hear about another way and we actually listen, we'll have our soul ripped right out of our jeans. Not a pretty sight. Ripped up in a thousand pieces. Ugly.

But if we're so sure of what we believe, why are we so threatened by *other* ideas?

Other ideas about God, love, grace, salvation, life, death, purpose, and meaning.

What scares us so much about being simply open? To the chance that God might speak to us in many ways. In different places, contexts, histories, cultures, times, and people.

What if we took a chance and read about a different way? We don't *have* to change our minds about anything. Really. But we might. We may not have new questions for God. But we might. We don't have to add something new to our core beliefs. But we might.

We don't have to truly wrestle and learn through it. But it might not be bad for us.

And we won't be torn into a thousand pieces, flung by a jealous God who needs it 'God's' way. Or the highway. That's helpful to know, especially when we suffer.

When we're tempted to circle the wagons and form a tighter knot around what we know.

And believe. And to foreclose anything else that causes us to wonder, question, or think.

In truth, wondering, questioning, or thinking in new ways may be the *very* best thing we can actually do. When we suffer. When we fight the urge to have it only one way.

Movement Seven:
Living with Silence

We have talk radio. Talk shows. Talking heads. Talking robo-calls.

We're talked at until we're blue in the face, exhausted, talked out, talked over.

And we talk back, talk to, talk with, talk at, and talk about. Especially the 'talk about'.

Silence is not golden. Not even silver or bronze. Not even a consolation prize.

Fill the airways, fill the void, fill the space, fill the conversation. Please, no silence.

It makes us uneasy, self-conscious, anxious. Like we want to get away from it.

We even fill our church services with sound. To the brim. Literally every moment of it. Preaching and hymns and prayers and readings. Top it off. Fill it, brother. All the way.

We have a problem with silence. With simply sitting. With emptying ourselves.

We even talk to ourselves . . . . and sometimes answer ourselves . . . or even argue.

But what if silence was not the enemy, the dark night of emptiness? What if we silently prayed to God? And allowed God to simply sit with us. No talk. Just sit together, like two old friends who didn't need language to know what the other is thinking. Like a long-married couple that simply enjoys 'being' together after all these years. Simply sitting together holding hands.

What if silence was not God's rejection of our prayers, ourselves, our plight, or our hopes? But simply a chance to get closer without the normal level of noise. A chance to break away from the 'ask-receive-ask again' cycle of our relationship with God.

It's hard to simply sit with God, especially when we need something from God. Especially when we're suffering. And the silence is deafening.

But what if that silence gave us a deeper sense of God's real presence, not simply God's presents? God's love, not simply God's loving gifts. God's life in us.

Movement Eight:
Living Descriptively

"The pain is awful. Really awful. Rotten."

"My nurse is mean. He's mean to me. He may be evil. I need a new nurse."

"This is the worst possible outcome for me. I can't think of anything more hopeless."

"They aren't telling me the truth about my illness. They're lying to me. How can they?"

We like to think of things in binary terms—either good or bad. Great or rotten.

Evil or saintly. Positive or negative. Powerful or weak. Glass full or empty.

But what about half-full or half-empty? What about none of the above?

Putting a label on things often seems like the way to go. It's easy, fast, and neat.

It quickly puts everything onto one pile or another. Sorts it all out. This pile or that one.

It's easier to do, but it's not that helpful. Especially when we suffer.

It gives us false fears, false hopes, false assuredness, false closure, and false simplicity.

Because, to be fair, things are rarely this *or* that. And they're rarely just good or bad.

Life is much more nuanced than that. Nearly all the time.

What if we *described* things and feelings, not labeled them so absolutely? Carefully and thoughtfully defined them, using better words about them. And their impact on us.

Without labels, quick judgments, or any judgment, really.

But by stepping back a few feet from it. Looking at it more objectively. Descriptively.

By naming what it feels like, looks like, sounds like to me. Descriptively. Specifically.

This is how it makes me feel, or act, or not act. Descriptively. Not judgmentally.

And let's talk about how we can work through those things. Descriptively. Together.

Letting go of what's 'worked for us for so long' is tough. Especially when we hurt.

Unless it never really worked for us after all. We just thought it did. But it didn't.

Movement Nine:
Living with Prayerfulness

"This is how to pray. Listen closely. Follow the instructions.

You thank God for everything God's given you. You then ask for God's mercy for all the bad stuff you've done. Then you ask God for what you want and need. Then you tell God you have faith that God will come through for you. Really come through this time. Then you say thanks again, God. Over and out, God. Just do it that way. That'll do it."

. . . Or you simply read your prayers from some 'how-to' book. "Follow the script."

. . . Or you sit quietly and focus on God's love, a word, or an object.

"Breathe. Focus. Quiet. No distractions. Others can join you. But keep it centered."

But when we're suffering, it's hard to do any of that. Yeah, focus. Right.

And the distractions part. Forget about that. "I've got people swarming all over me. And I have the incessant beeps of this machine that monitors my heart, pulse rate, and breathing." Or the machine that breathes for me. Or helps me breath. Or I'm too out of breath to pray. Or I can't cause I'm crying or groaning. And don't have the words today.

So, what if we thought about our prayers differently? Really differently.

What if our tears and our laughter and our anger were praying to God in some way?

Our conversations with others. Our times of loving silence with a spouse or friend.

Holding hands with a loved one. Or even a stranger . . . who took the time to care.

What if prayer was primarily a means of connecting us with others? And with God.

Like a giant network of virtual wires and transmitters. Without all the Hardware.

Only Software, really. Software. And with only one Application: communicating in love with each other and with our Creator.

With or without words. For God already knows anyway . . .

Movement Ten:
Living Mindfully

"Sit quietly. Close your eyes. Clear your mind. Breathe.

Listen to the sound of your breath. Listen as it goes slowly in and out. Listen.

Feel your breath coming up from your diaphragm. Feel the sense of exhaling.

Then slowly inhale, feeling your insides fill with air. Listen for your breath."

It's not easy finding a quiet place in this noisy world. It's hard to clear our cluttered minds. It's even harder to keep our eyes closed. Harder yet to focus on something as simple as our breathing. Nearly impossible to unplug completely and sit with ourselves.

When we're aching and suffering, it's even harder. And we don't much feel like it.

Our troubled minds wander everywhere after only a few minutes. Then we add another item to our list. The list of things we need to do now to feel better. The long one.

But what if simply 'being' in the moment was more important than 'doing'? Especially when 'doing' is precisely the only thing we think we should do. Resist the temptation.

Consider the counter-intuitive thing: not doing for a change. For a moment.

Simply be in the moment. For a moment. Simply quiet your mind and soul.

For a moment. And do so mindfully. For a moment. For yourself.

When we let go of yesterday and tomorrow and even today for a moment . . .

We're more mindfully 'in' this moment. The one that counts most. The one that might heal the most. The one that might comfort the most. The one that might love the most.

What if you set aside time each day for only yourself and some quiet? And for God.

It might be the very moment when God strengthens, guides, forgives, loves, and heals.

When emptying yourself creates real space in you for something new from God.

A gift. A peace. A way. A friend. A God-hug. For you. In you. In that moment.

Movement Eleven:
Living with Your True Self

Most of us don't live well with ourselves. We think we do, but we don't.

We live the life of someone we'd rather be. The one that others prefer we had.

The one we read and dream about. Hear about. Saw on TV. Saw at the movies.

Not the one we really have. Not the real one. Not the one we're ashamed of.

The one that believes the untrue stories of others about us. The one that wishes we were thinner, prettier, smarter, wiser, richer, healthier, happier. Because we heard from someone else that we should 'be' those things. And we bought the farm on all that stuff. Bought it. Accepted it. Welcomed it in. Asked it to stay.

"Come on in . . . Yes, come in." Not just for a night, or a week, or a month. Nope. A long-term lease.

Then we took it all and took ourselves way too seriously. Then quit laughing, except at ourselves. Not the 'laugh with' kind of laugh. But rather the one where we're laughing 'at' ourselves. The mean, self-loathing kind of laugh. And in the process, we cut ourselves off from ourselves, from others, from our world, and from God. And then we got sick or lost someone. The laughing turned to crying. Sobbing. Loud sobbing.

But what if we stopped listening to all that noise? Even the self-inflicted racket.

Or at least quit inviting it in all the time. What if we stood back from it?

Looked at it more dispassionately and objectively? Decided how much of it we wanted to believe or accept, or act on, or even 'own'. Decided what we want to keep.

Then decided what we want to toss out. Like the stuff that isn't true. And the stuff that isn't healthy for us. That's not in our best interest. Others just think it is.

What if we spent more time believing in ourselves? Our true, best, more-well selves.

What if living better with ourselves actually helped to make us feel better? Way better.

Movement Twelve:
Living with Goodbyes

Sometimes things don't work out as we planned, we hoped, we prayed for, we longed for.

Sometimes friends and family die, leave us, get hurt and don't get fully well.

Sometimes we lose our jobs, our livelihoods, our homes, our retirement, and our savings.

Sometimes the story doesn't end with the words, "And I lived happily ever after."

Sometimes things don't work out as I wanted them to. Or believed they would.

And we need to say 'goodbye' to someone, something, some place, or some dream.

Maybe for a week, or the time being, or awhile. Sometimes forever. Or so it seems.

It may be the hardest thing we've *ever* had to do. Or will ever do again. Ever.

But in truth, we begin saying 'goodbye' from the very moment we're born.

We say 'goodbye' to summers, falls, winters, and springs. To places or things.

To our childhood, our innocence, our idealism, our friend, our figure, and our hair.

All things have their seasons. All things have their times. All things.

We mark those seasons and times and people. We remember. We memorialize.

We move forward as best we can. We say 'goodbye'. But do we really?

The most beautiful leaves are in the fall. Their radiant red, yellow, and orange colors splash the clear, autumn skies. Like magnificent paintings on canvas. And then they fall from the tree. They appear to brown and to wither and to die. Dead leaves . . .

And they say 'goodbye' to us. And leave us forever. But do they really?

In truth, they seed the fallow, winter soil. They stir the ground that's nourished and moved by them. Then bring forth new life in the spring. Because of the fallen leaves. The ones we said 'goodbye' to last fall. Or thought we did. Everything has a season.

What if 'goodbye' was simply 'so long' to what is now? And not 'goodbye' forever.

Movement Thirteen: Living with God

"When my illness began, everything changed for me. Everything was different.

I wasn't able to walk, do, or care for myself anymore. I lost my independence. My dignity. My privacy. My abilities. I lost nearly everything that I valued most."

But what if we valued *someone* more than all those things we valued most and felt we'd lost? What if we valued most the *One* Person who wants *us* more than anything else?

The very God who has made us, cared for us, nurtured us, powered us, forgiven us, and loved us. Even when we're truly unreachable and unlovable. I mean truly unruly.

The very God who never stopped on us, never walked away from us, never gave up on us. Even when we gave up on ourselves or on God. Truly quit. Even when we ignored God. Even when we turned away. When we truly said, 'Get lost, Dude. Yeah, you God.'"

Suffering knows no seasons. It happens in all of them. It happens to everyone.

It's a mystery that we have no one ready, easy, snappy, simple answer for.

But one thing brings comfort. In the silence, reflection, contemplation, and prayer of suffering, God is present. A God who cares, who heals and comforts, who brings things and people to help, who suffers with, who never leaves. If only we'll believe.

For at the very moment when faith in God seems the hardest thing to have . . .

God is most ready to enter. Imperceptibly. Quietly. With a whisper. With a clang. With a song. With a smile. With a hug or a kiss. With a vision. With a plan.

With a friend. With a companion. A Divine companion. The Divine One.

With the Divine, listening ear. With a kind and gentle Divine hand. With a warm and loving Divine embrace. With a comforting, Divine word for us.

One who brings a lasting and an everlasting loving hope. Who simply 'Brings It'.

Movement Fourteen:
Living Everlasting 'Hell-Free'

"Hell." There, I said it. The bad place. The really, really hot place. Bad hot.

For bad people. For those guys. The bad guys. Even the good guys that don't think right. The ones who do the right things, but don't believe right. Right. Wrong. Gone.

In my faith tradition, we talk about Hell, we think about Hell, we fear Hell.

We dread spending forever in Hell. We wonder if we're going to Hell.

Sometimes, we're warned about Hell. If we don't think right. Live right. Believe right.

Now, it's bad enough to have this hanging over our heads when things are going right.

When we suffer, it's even worse. And it's not right. Especially then.

But what if things weren't that simple after all? What if it isn't an 'either-or' after all?

We are loved. We are forgiven. But we are also accountable. Our actions matter.

We create a little bit of heaven when we love others. We give them hell when we don't.

Some moments in our lives feel almost like heaven. Others feel like pure hell.

So, what if heaven and hell were really most about here? And not the hereafter.

What if our job here was to love God and love others? Spread heaven. Beat back hell.

Help lift others from their hells. While helping them to enjoy a little more heaven.

To work with God and with each other to build a more lasting Heaven. Everlasting.

And when we die, to sit with God and fully understand our very own prior, living hells.

Those we made for ourselves. Or for others. Or because of others. Or for no reason.

And what if God made those hells go away? Disappear forever. All the bad stuff.

But kept the good stuff. Our good light. Our good acts. Our good effects.

To be used now and in the future Reign. By God. Along with those of others.

With the perfect, discerning vision that only God can have. 20/20 Heaven vision.

Movement Fifteen:
Living with Joy

Happy, happy, happy, happy, happy.

"I'm sure happy about how it all turned out. Happy that we've got this one done."

"I'm so happy for your new promotion, Mary. Really great news. Really happy."

"I'm very happy about our vacation this year. The weather really cooperated."

"I'm extremely happy right now. Everything's going my way these days."

Happy, happy, happy, happy, happy. Happy . . . until they're not anymore.

"I'm terribly unhappy at the moment. Everything's working against me these days."

On some days, we're feeling happy. Ecstatic. On others, we're not. Miserable.

Especially when we're suffering. Hard to feel happy about that. Maybe impossible.

But what if we can still have joyfulness . . . even in the face of pain and sorrow? Possible.

Joyfulness isn't the same as happiness. Joy's grounded on a deep, abiding sense of peace and purpose in our lives. On a deeper meaning. On a deeper hope. A deeper connection.

Grounded in knowing who we are. What we are. Why we're really here on earth.

For life throws some nasty things our way. Truth. And it's hard to be happy with them.

But joy runs deeper. Has real staying power. No matter what.

Even when the bad stuff keeps on coming. Even when a bad day runs on. Longer.

Into a bad week. Into a bad month. A bad year. Maybe a bad decade, even.

Cherish and enjoy the happy moments in our lives. That's what they are. Moments.

Celebrate them. Dance with them. Smile and laugh with them. Be grateful for them.

But you can't 'live' on them. Cause they're fleeting. They won't last. Bad stuff will come. Sure as you breathe or stand there. Sure as you think they won't. They will.

And when they do, hold onto joy. You'll get a lasting peace and comfort in return.

Movement Sixteen:
Living with Hope

'Hope'. When this word seems furthest away, don't give it up. Hope. When all seems lost, don't give it up. Hope. When there's no reason to go on, don't give it up.

Hope. When *they* say, "It's terminal. He's gone. We couldn't save her. Your divorce is now final. I'm sorry, but we have to lay you off. We can't offer you this position. I don't want to go out with you anymore. I'm leaving you. I never really loved you."

Hope. When *you* say, "I'm moving away from everyone I've ever loved. I'm worried sick. I'm afraid. I'm terrified at the prospect of this. I'm completely lost right now. I'm alone. I can't take another step. I don't know where to turn." Hope even then.

Hope that it will somehow all work out in the end . . . even if I'm no longer here to see it. Even if I can't imagine how. Hope that the end is not really the end. It might just be a beginning of something else. Hope when all signs point to no hope whatsoever.

Hope in God who created a world where *all* things and *all* lives are forever sacred.

Hope in Christ Jesus who came down to us, not to die for us, but to show us what it really looks like to live and die with unconditional love, grace, courage, trust . . . and hope.

Hope in the Spirit who breaths for, prays for, and holds us up. Who empowers us to love and forgive others. To serve others who suffer—and to stay with them and listen to them and share their pain with them. And go well beyond feeling sorry for them.

Hope for life squarely in the midst of death. Hope for Heaven in the midst of Hell.

Hope for new life, promise, and purpose. Out of the ashes of suffering and emptiness.

Hope that lifts us from our pit of despair. That heals us in new, unexpected ways.

That brings us closer to God. That resurrects our spirit. That showers us with love.

That works. Today. Tomorrow. Next week. Next year. Next decade. Forever.

Post-Movement Reflection Questions

How can I create shifts in my life that demand less unnecessary precision, clarity, and surety?

What options have I unwittingly overlooked or closed off in my journey of suffering? In what ways can I look to the future of change with greater creativity and openness?

How can I learn to see communion with God more holistically in each moment of the day? How can I become less rigid in my definitions of prayer in the process?

What if I stopped reacting so quickly and negatively to situations of suffering? Then stood back from it with greater objectivity, descriptiveness, and specificity—rather than simply labeling it as 'good' or 'bad'?

How would my life change if I let go of my fear of Hell and eternal damnation? Then lived today more fully in God's life and love—sitting right inside of me forever? How might that create greater hope and joy for me?

Post Movement Rest and Prayer

Loving God, thank you for the many things that help me to move on. Move forward. Move with more purpose. Move with new meaning. Even in the midst of my suffering. Thank you for the many questions that I live with, even when I'd really prefer more answers. Please help me to find truth and revelation in those questions—even the ones that aren't ever answered here. Help me to live this path of suffering with openness to possibilities. Not just to my losses. Help me to see lasting life even in the face of impermanence. Help me to explore the options before me, not simply the ones now closed off. Help me to see you more clearly in all things, in myself, and in others. Help me to see and hear you more clearly, even in apparent periods of silence. Help me to pray when I can't or don't feel like it anymore. Help me to see that my tears, my fears and doubts, my hopes, my stories, and my time with others are all prayers to you. They keep me connected in love with you. Help me to live more mindfully and in the moment. That I might see you in that space. In that time. Right now. Most of all, God, may I live in and through all things squarely in your presence. May I live with the knowledge that my real purpose on earth is to love you and others. To live with you and others in joy, peace, and communion. In so doing, might I bring to others some little bit of Heaven right here—even in the face of the hells that my suffering brings in this moment. For the things of hell are not of you, God. They are not by you. You are, rather, the true embodiment and hope of Heaven. Both now and in the future. Both here and in all places.

The Heaven of Life. Of Love. Of Grace. Of Communion. A Heaven worth hoping for. Truly hoping for. Thank you, God.

Chapter Eight

Finding The End of the Island

"What lies behind us and what lies before us are tiny matters compared to what lies within us."

—RALPH WALDO EMERSON

Movement One:
Concluding the Story

The old man's pace had slowed considerably in the past few days. He found himself out of breath more often. He sat down more often. He rested more often. He stopped more often. He saw his own decline more readily, more often. He thought more deeply more often. He sensed the nearing end more often. Nearing the end of the island that he had so intently sought over the past few weeks. Maybe then he'd know one thing more fully. The reason for his pain. The reason for his suffering. The reason for his many losses during his long, lonely life. Something to hold firmly onto. Some reason that might explain it all. To make things clearer for him. Then he would leave the island and go home. "Just make it to the end—whenever and wherever it is," he said to himself as he dragged along.

The old man walked. Then he rested. And slept. Then he walked again. Ever slower. But he wasn't bothered by the urgency of it all as much as before. His sense that 'time was short' wasn't so present to him any longer. The need to push on, to push ahead, or to make it somewhere wasn't as pronounced. In its place, he felt a stronger sense of space, of others, and of life about him. He smelled the things around him more. He relished the taste of things more. He took greater peace in the touch of things, the sound of things, and feel of others. The wind in his face seemed gentler. The warmth of the sun was more comforting. The cool of the breeze was more refreshing. The sounds of the birds were sweeter. The water before him was more soothing. The night sky was more relaxing. The moon was more inviting.

The old man woke later in the morning than usual on this day. He walked to the pond near him and rinsed his face. The coolness of this water brought him a sense of brisk awakening. Today would be a good day, he thought, as he rose from kneeling at the water's edge. Perhaps, today he might find the end of the island. Maybe not, but maybe nonetheless. He wiped his brow with his now tattered and wrinkled shirt. He gathered himself for today's walk, and headed up the path before him. After walking for some time, he looked ahead more intently into a clearing beyond a short ridge. His heart raced a little at the prospect of his journey's end. His breathing quickened and he tried to calm himself. He didn't want to be disappointed by a mirage. The man wiped his brow again and said to himself, "Steady, old man. Don't get your hopes up, here. Just keep walking. We'll see what we see in a minute or two. Steady."

But as he neared the clearance, his heart danced and leapt. In his old, weary bones, the old man sensed that something was really different on this day. He somehow knew that he approached someplace that mattered. That mattered more than any place to-date on this island. Something was different about this. He knew it, even if he didn't. He scanned left, then right, then straight ahead. Something different. But also something vaguely like he'd seen before. Something that was strangely familiar, but he couldn't place it exactly. He pushed faster toward the clearance. It came closer ahead. This was it. He knew it. This was his hope. This was his day. His time to finally know. Now.

The man reached the ridge and gazed urgently at the place just ahead. His expectant, hopeful smile melted suddenly and abruptly away. Like molten lava rushing from an exploding volcano. Like a burning sensation of a raging fire. Like the sense that his hot blood was quickly draining from his face . . . and onto the ground. Gone. He could now hardly stand under the weight of the horror that he gazed upon. The man saw his glimmer of hope dash violently away. He tried to steady himself. "Look away from this," he said to himself. "Look to the horizon." But the landscape before his eyes lost its color. The sharp lines of the trees blurred. The brilliant blue of the morning skies washed out. The rocky coastline was now shrouded before him in a fog. Lifeless. Voided. Gone. An aching emptiness and void. The old man dropped to his shaky knees. Then his heavy body fell like a rock to the ground. He wanted it all to simply end now. It was over.

The man lay lifeless for what seemed like some hours. He resisted opening his eyes. But warm tears forced the eyes to create space for their flow. The new wetness on his face caused sand to stick to it. As if the insult of his discovery was now made worse by the coarseness of his skin. For a moment, he welcomed the sandy layer on his cheek. If only he could hide forever behind these grains of sand. Perhaps no one would recognize him any longer. Perhaps he wouldn't recognize himself either. Perhaps he could leave his own body forever. Or hide behind his new mask of sand.

The old man was rustled by the sound of a few others. As they drew nearer, the sound of their voices quickened and heightened. He wanted them to go away, but he couldn't muster the strength to project his now lifeless, voiceless voice. Then he felt his right shoulder being lifted. Then felt his body leaving the ground. Then heard the voice of another, "Let us help you up, old man. Don't worry. We'll get you up." The man didn't want to be lifted up. He wanted to simply lay face down. But the force of many kind hands brought him to his knees. Then to his feet. Steadied by the firm hands of a handful of strangers.

The small group of strangers dusted the sand and dirt from the old man's clothes. They gently rubbed the sand from his face and eyes. Then brushed it out of his hair. Straightened his shirt and wiped his shoes. The man mustered his remaining energy. He wavered between saying "thank you" and pleading with them to "leave me alone." He wasn't sure which, so he said nothing. One of the strangers asked, "Glad we found you here. Glad we found you so quickly. What happened to you, old man?" The man returned a stoic stare. He answered only out of some measure of courtesy. And replied, "I found the end of the island. And I know now that there isn't an end after all. No answer to my suffering. I walked and searched for weeks and weeks. I can't remember how long anymore. I followed the path from the beginning. I never strayed from it. And it ends here. Here. Not at the end. But here, where I began. 'There' is now 'here'. The end of the island is nothing more than the start of the island. I came here to find the answer at the end of this place. Yet I end at where I actually came from, still seeking the answer. I didn't walk a path. I walked a circle." The old man quietly sobbed.

The strangers gently placed the man on a level rock on the beach. One of them sat quietly with him for nearly an hour. As time passed, others joined. They sat together without words. As the old man gathered himself, he now vaguely recollected their faces. He began to put these 'new' faces with those of strangers who had joined him along his recent journey. He recalled their brief encounters together. The conversations. The things said. The things shared. The things discovered. Together. His gathering mind was nudged by a question from one of the strangers. She asked, "So, what now for you?" The man responded, "I guess I'll keep moving. Not sure to where exactly. But I'll keep moving somewhere forward." The stranger smiled and replied, "And we'll be here as you do so." She asked the old man, "I'm curious. What have you learned so far that can help you as you journey on?" The old man thought on that for some moments. In truth, he didn't need to think for long. He had reflected on that very thing for much of his time throughout the weeks before. He turned to the stranger and offered, "I learned that it's better to go with the power of the wind than to fight continuously against it. To look for shelter from it where I can. To let go more easily. To love myself more. To let others love and help me more. To see power a little differently. To look for life in new places. To see that endings are just as beautiful as beginnings. And sometimes, they are just that. To orient myself in relationship with others, not by myself. To go with the wind at my back. To follow the currents. To stop more along the way. To simply take it all in more often. To find hope in mystery and moments and questions, not just in answers. For, sometimes there aren't any. In all of it, I guess I feel loved most of all. I feel like I've never really been alone. Even when I thought I was."

One stranger smiled and said, "I guess none of us have. We were all like you when we came here. We came to find the answer and leave. Just like you. But we didn't get the answer we were looking for. Instead, we got more questions, more paradoxes, and more mysteries to contemplate on. But we learned from them. Maybe that's what keeps us moving, after all." The stranger knelt before the old man and gently hugged him. She offered, "So, we'll see you down the path." The man came back, "Perhaps. I think I feel better now. But I'm tired. I think I'll sleep for awhile." The strangers said their 'goodbyes'. Then they parted ways along the path.

The old man sat in place for a while. He became lost in his thoughts. Thoughts about the island. About the end that really wasn't an end in the end. About what he'd learned along the way. He didn't find the end. But he also realized something else. That he found something more important in the process: Himself. He found a bit more of himself in the end. Not at the end. But in the end. And he came to know that *this* was what mattered most. The man's eyes were heavy now. But the weight on him seemed lighter. He felt a little disappointment, to be sure. But he also felt peace. Not the resigned kind of peace. But, rather, an abiding, more hopeful one. He would rest now for a while. Tomorrow, he would walk on. He then closed his eyes. And fell into a deep sleep. He dreamed that a gentle hand reached for him. A loving hand. A peace-filled, grace-filled hand. An inviting, embracing hand. The old man took that hand. And was led gently away. Then the old man peacefully, almost imperceptibly breathed his last. He lay on the sand, gone. He left a smile behind.

Some days later, another boat arrived. Five new passengers disembarked. A curious mix of old and young. Men and women. Frail and strong. They were met by a stranger, who welcomed each of them. When asked what brought them here, they said they sought the end of the island. They were looking for an answer to their suffering. An answer to their pain. An answer to their losses. The kind stranger turned toward them and asked, "How did you know that you might find the answer here?" One of the new arrivals smiled. She said, "We found some bottles on our beaches back home. Many, many miles away. We found a different message in each bottle. Apparently from an old man here. About the 'answers' that he found. Right here. On the island. They weren't really answers, I guess. More about what he was learning. About his suffering. But also about himself. His thoughts beckoned us to come ourselves. In a compelling, provocative kind of way. It was like he was calling us. And so we're here. To find the answers. Or the questions. Or something in-between."

The stranger extended her hand to those of the new arrivals. She pointed to the path before them. And she offered, "Take this path. That's the one. The one to the end of the island." They thanked the stranger and turned toward the path. One of them offered, "Thank you, friend. We'd love to talk some more, but time is short. We need to find the end of the island. But, if you see the old man who sent the notes in the bottles, please thank him for us. We greatly appreciate his wisdom." The stranger replied, "I will. I'm sure I'll be seeing him around. Yes, I'm sure I'll be seeing him around." They waved and departed down the path.

Two months later, ten more passengers disembarked on the island. Four months later, fifty more came. Then a hundred more . . . They kept coming. And searching. And growing. And living. Embracing movement for its own sake. With or without an 'end'.

Postscript

Next to the Bible and the many theology texts that I've studied through the years, perhaps no writing has inspired my thinking more than Oscar Wilde's *The Happy Prince*. While not a Christian or a salvation story, per se, this book has taught me much about our human meaning and purpose in this world. The story recounts the meeting of a southerly migrating Swallow and a statue of a Happy Prince at the outset of winter. The statue had once been a young boy, sequestered within a garden estate where everything he saw was beautiful. Now, as a statue at the entrance to the city, he has experienced for the first time the misery of poverty and sickness all around him. He is crying.

He befriends the Swallow, convincing the bird, however reluctantly at first, to stay with him and remove the rubies, sapphires, and gold plating from the Happy Prince's statue-body to provide them to the suffering poor in the city. As winter sets in, the Prince's loyal friend, the Swallow, dies of cold (but in service) at the feet of the statue. The now shabby statue is torn down and melted. However, the statue's heart will not melt down, and is discarded along with the dead Swallow into the trash. God asks an angel to bring to God the most precious things in the city. The angel returns with the dead Swallow and the Happy Prince's lead heart. God proclaims that, in God's garden of paradise, the Swallow will now sing for everyone. The Happy Prince will praise God's name forever.

This beloved story was written many, many years ago. It survives and continues to inspire today. Perhaps its power is most influenced by the scandal that surrounded its author. Oscar Wilde was highly proclaimed as a literary genius. He lived and lavished in the high society of his day. But he was later excoriated for his sexuality amidst derision and taunting. He died a forgotten nobody, someone on the fringe of 'acceptable' society. By all logical definition, he died marginalized and alone. He suffered the worst kind of pain and loss, I'm sure. But perhaps his heart refused to melt down in the ashes. I pray that, in all he faced, his heart didn't melt. His story has survived and has thrived. So has his heart. Even to the End of the Island.

I have used the backdrop of The Happy Prince numerous times in my writings through the years. A fellow chaplain once commented to me that my own pastoral identity might be closely linked to the prince in the story. Since that moment of insight, I have wondered at times whether I might, in fact, be the happy prince. In many ways, I have stood outside the intense suffering of poverty, want, marginalization, and isolation that countless others face in their lives. But I have also gently strived to enter into this space and offer all that I can. I hope that I have given my own suffering and wounds in ways that make me more authentic, compassionate, and present to others. I pray that I will continue to offer to others the God-given gifts of rubies and emeralds plated onto my 'statue'. As the years pass, I will surely wear down and rust. So must we all.

But while I may have an end here on earth, I trust that, on the Island we call life, there is no 'End' per se. The paths that crisscross the Island simply round the block of sorts. And God is always there along the way, saying, "Welcome home, my child. Welcome home." As I walk my own island, my fervent prayer and hope is this: With God's everlasting love, grace, and welcome, I pray that my own heart will be just like that of the Happy Prince. It will live for others. It will cry for others. It will be given for others. And it will be shared for others. But I pray that it will never melt down. May it never melt down. Instead, may it be returned to God one day, intact, strong, and still working.

God bless you all.

With Infinite Gratitude

Next to God, I count my relationship with my wife, Carmen, as my closest and dearest. Carmen and I met in college, and dated exclusively with each other until we were subsequently married after our graduations. Throughout our lives together, she has unconditionally believed in me, encouraged me, forgiven me, and loved me. I consider her the love of my life, my soul mate, and my best friend. We started careers together, homes together, and a family together. She is the mother of our two children, the next greatest blessing in our lives. She has blessed not only their lives and mine, but also those of countless other children, as a school teacher for many years.

Carmen is responsible for helping to bring me back to the faith and for supporting my journey to seminary at mid-life. She has stood by me during my many long hours of study and classes away from home. She has been infinitely patient with me as I tried to balance work and study with my most crucial role as husband and father. Perhaps most importantly, though, she's encouraged me to write—specifically, to write this book. In fact, the name of the book, *The End of the Island*, is her idea. She shared it with me some years ago while we were traveling along the Eastern Shore of the Chesapeake Bay, a place that we treasure together. While I thank the Chesapeake for the naming inspiration, I thank my wife, Carmen, for her daily inspiration. For her daily love. For simply being the incredible, special person that she is. She is not an Island. And there is no End to her Heart. No End to her Love. They begin Anew Each Day. Like that of God . . . Amen.